Informing Innovation:

Tracking Student Interest in Emerging Library Technologies at Ohio University

Char Booth

Foreword by
Joan K. Lippincott

Association of College & Research Libraries
A Division of the American Library Association
Chicago 2009

Table of Contents

List of Illustrations

List of Illustrations

Foreword

I believe that this Research Report is a "must read" for academic librarians. Char Booth has succeeded in providing us with a snapshot of the major issues involved in thinking through Web 2.0 services in academic libraries, as well as a model for implementing a local research design in order to better understand your own institution's users' needs.

On first reading this manuscript, the two words that came to mind were "insightful" and "thoughtful." Booth has a keen understanding of social networking technologies, especially in the context of library services, and she does not accept platitudes or surface perceptions of their value or success. She examines the implementation of new technologies in libraries in a way that makes us see them with fresh perspective. Her critical view elucidates why some efforts have succeeded and why others have failed. She delves into issues deeply in order to improve our understanding of the relationships between library users, information, and technology.

How much of what we know about and read about the current generation of students and their use of technology is hype and stereotype, and how much is based in fact? Do undergraduates or Net Gen students on our campuses have a special relationship with technology that we need to address in the services we offer in libraries? Char makes the case that much of the way we develop services should be based on a genuine understanding of our local user populations.

The broad context that Booth illustrates includes a candid description of the range of library implementations of various Web 2.0 services and the successes and failures that have resulted. Her analysis of the literature of Net Gen students, technology use in higher education, and library use would make excellent background reading for an academic library retreat for strategic planning. She brings all of this knowledge to bear in her description of the student-focused environmental library and technology scan she spearheaded during her time at Ohio University.

I hope that many institutions will benefit from the way in which Char describes the thought process that went into developing the methodology for her study. It is all too easy for librarians in academic institutions to embark on putting together a survey without doing the deep background work she documents in this Research Report. As academic librarians, it is incumbent on us to deploy rigorous methodology practices, which Booth describes so well. Her explanation of the many elements that should be considered when embarking on a survey, including using campus data gathered for other purposes, working with campus partners on survey or other instrument development, and considering a variety of methodologies, is a good roadmap for others. She provides a highly useful and concise tutorial on many aspects of research design. Part I provides the context of the study and the overall considerations of its design and implementation, while Part II presents findings and analysis of the data.

It is no surprise to me that ALA has recognized Char Booth in its Emerging Leaders program and that *Library Journal* named her a "Mover and Shaker" in 2008. Her abilities to analyze and synthesize a wide body of literature and keep up with the latest trends are masterful. A natural writer, she can describe complex processes in very clear prose. Her energy and her optimism for the role of academic librarians are contagious. I hope Char Booth's work will inform your own process for better understanding the technology needs of your user community. In addition, I encourage you to have a virtual collaborative learning experience with Char by reading and responding to her blog at infomational.wordpress.com; I know I will be doing that myself.

Joan K. Lippincott

Chair, *ACRL New Publications Advisory Board*
Associate Executive Director, *Coalition for Networked Information*

Acknowledgements

I dedicate this project to my friends and former coworkers at Ohio University in Athens, Ohio, who prove how effective academic libraries can become through flexibility, teamwork, and a clear focus on the user experience. Their energy, collegiality, and humor are rightly becoming legendary, and the creativity and responsiveness of the OU Libraries should be a model to all. Although I have since relocated, I hope this report is testament to the extraordinary mentorship and inspiration I received there during my first years as a librarian.

Thanks to everyone at Alden Library who made this project possible - my Technology Team colleagues: Chad Boeninger, Chris Guder, Tim Smith, and Mike Wilson; the entire Reference and Instruction Department: Wanda Weinberg, Marne Grinolds, Jessica Hagman, Derek Malone, Sherri Saines, Cathy Sitko, Jessica Stith, Steve Steward, Andrew Stuart, Lorraine Wochna, and Jason Whited, also former Dean of Libraries, Julia Zimmerman, and Assistant Dean of Collections and Access, Jan Maxwell. Special gratitude to Chris Guder for collaborating with me on the ACRL 2009 conference version of this research, and to Dean of Libraries Scott Seaman for first encouraging me to publish these findings.

My gratitude and respect to Kathryn Deiss and Joan Lippincott at ACRL, with whom I have had the distinct privilege of working closely on this project and whose interest and insights have been indispensable. Special thanks to Kathryn for being an amazingly creative and flexible editor and friend. I am also indebted to Jennifer Dorner, Pat Maughan, Wanda Weinberg, Chris Guder, and Scott Seaman for their support and eleventh-hour editorial input. Warmest thanks to OU College of Education professor Sandra Turner for her enthusiastic mentorship - godspeed for a swift recovery - and also to my father and stepmother, John Booth and Patti Richard, for their support and statistical acumen (just my luck to have faculty in the family). Gratitude to all my new colleagues at UC Berkeley, far too numerous to list, for giving me such an excellent welcome, and to my former UT Austin colleagues, because it still only feels like I left yesterday. Deep thanks to Leslie Dreyer for her patience, humor, and design input, and to my mother, Julie Stillwell, and sister, Caroline Lara, for being generally amazing.

Last but not least, my fiercest appreciation to UCSD librarian/friend/collaborator/editor extraordinaire Lia Friedman, as always, for neither pulling punches nor twirling skirts where my writing (or anything else) is concerned. Thank you for making this better.

Introduction: Testing Technolust

Like many others, over the past several years the Ohio University Libraries has experimented with emerging social, mobile, and dynamic technologies in order to develop a more responsive range of student-focused services. The Reference and Instruction Department at Alden Library has been recognized for its innovative work with Skype reference, library wikis, customized browser toolbars, interactive FAQ knowledgebases, and video reference kiosks. Also like many others, we learned that maintaining and assessing front-line technologies is a demanding iterative process that requires long-term resource allocation and personal commitment from many stakeholders. And always, a nagging question remained – if we build this, will our students care?

Mixed results with several of our more experimental programs led the OU Libraries' Technology Team to diagnose a local case of what Michael Stephens has described as "technolust," or the creation of library technologies for their own sake, based on the assumption that they are inherently needed and desired (2008). Finding ourselves spread increasingly thin in our ability to develop new services while supporting existing ones, we determined that actual user needs and expectations should be more effectively incorporated into the planning and evaluation process. In order to create services that better contributed to the overall library experience, we needed to understand how students actually interacted with libraries and technology, instead of how we assumed that they did.

This report examines one institution's efforts to move away from technolust toward what many have described as a "culture of assessment" (Lakos & Phipps, 2004, Farkas, 2008). In collaboration with the OU Libraries Technology Team, I led a large-scale environmental scanning initiative in the Winter and Spring quarters of 2008 that investigated the factors that motivate student interest in emerging library technologies. Environmental scans identify underlying trends that affect an institution and the way it is perceived by its users, thereby providing a sense of gestalt instrumental to making strategic and informed decisions. Our assessment of student library, information, and communication technology use consisted of two web-based surveys, both of which generated strong response rates (N1=3,648; N2=1,651). By researching student library perceptions in conjunction with their attitudes towards information, communication, and academic tools, I hoped to test the generational and demographic assumptions that influenced our local development of emerging public service technologies.

In the following chapters, I use data produced by the 2008 OU Libraries Student Technology Survey to explore the intersection of student technology and library cultures during a time of rapid sociotechnical change. I present a window into the demographic and academic connections between library perceptions and receptivity to emerging technologies. My examination illustrates the necessity of local user research, which provides insight into unique institutional cultures and student learning environments, and suggests how libraries can leverage collected data to both evaluate and prioritize a range of initiatives. While readers should consider these survey findings specific to the student population and institutional culture of the OU Libraries, they carry significant implications for technology development and evaluation on a broader scale.

To encourage local cultures of assessment at other academic libraries, I also offer insight into the process and product of practical user research. I critically examine the development, collection, and analysis phases of the Ohio University survey project, identifying caveats and pitfalls common to homegrown user assessment in academic libraries. I consider various types of research for their respective strengths and applications in a library context, provide a sample survey instrument template modeled on the questionnaires used in the Ohio University scan (Appendix A), and recommend additional data sources that can inform comprehensive local research strategies. By offering this analysis, my goal is to inspire similar attempts to gain deep contextual understanding of campus, student, and library cultures.

Organization

This report is presented in two parts. *Part One: Local Insight to Library Practice* (Chapters 1-3) analyzes the current climate of public service innovation in college and research libraries and considers how this process might be informed by strategies in user investigation. *Part Two: A Case Study in Environmental Scanning* (Chapters 4-8) presents the findings of the 2008 Ohio University Student Library Technology Survey, illustrating the span of information that can be gathered from comprehensive local research.

Chapter 1 examines the shifting influence of Library 2.0 and other factors that have guided recent attempts at technology development in academic libraries. Chapter 2 explores the literature concerning generational change, technology use, and student library perceptions in higher education. Chapter 3 considers best practices in environmental scanning, research collaboration, survey construction, marketing, and data analysis using the Ohio University project as a case study. Chapters 4-7 analyze closed and open-ended student responses regarding library, information, and technology use and perceptions. Chapter 8 concludes with a consideration of the programmatic implications of local research, offering recommendations regarding assessment cultures and the future of innovation in library user services.

Appendix A provides an updated and annotated survey instrument template modeled on the original OU questionnaires, which can be adapted to create or support similar environmental scanning projects. Appendix B is an example of a customized "student library/technology profile" of first-year respondents, created for OU's First-Year Outreach Librarian using the statistical software package SPSS using a process of rapid variable brainstorming and analysis described in Chapter 3. Appendix C outlines scales and measures used to conduct the correlation analyses in Chapters 4 and 7.

Note: Readers interested in scanning survey findings will find a description of research design and methodology in Chapter 3, a summary of participant demographics in Chapter 4, followed by a detailed discussion of findings in Chapters 5-7.

Definition of Terms

For the purposes of this report, *technology* describes internet applications, mobile devices, computer software and hardware, and other tools that enable communication, search, and media use/creation. *Information* refers to print and electronic resources accessible via the web, media, and library interfaces. *Web 2.0* describes dynamic, collaborative, and/or user-driven internet applications as well as the social and entrepreneurial movements that popularized them. Similarly, *Library 2.0* describes both the movement within librarianship calling for the integration of user-centered technology as well as a number of specific social and dynamic services. *Disruptive technologies* provide users with new ways of "networking, interfacing, and producing content," transforming existing markets and behaviors and causing older technologies to obsolesce (Burgleman, et al., 2007, para. 1). *Academic technologies* describe learning management systems (LMSs) and other instructional tools, whereas *personal learning environments* are the computer-based applications, and web interfaces uniquely configured by an individual to facilitate their own learning, i.e. Facebook, Google Documents, and/or Firefox extensions (Sclater, 2008); at times I extend Sclater's definition to include physical spaces, such as group study areas, learning/information commons, library carrels, or cafés. Everett Rogers' *technology adoption scale* distinguishes between late, mainstream, and early technology adopters (2003). *Academic status* is synonymous with academic standing, and describes the distinction between graduate, undergraduate, and non-degree seeking students. *Digital status* refers to Marc Prensky's age-based dichotomy of *digital natives* and *digital immigrants*, or individuals born before and after approximately 1980 with ostensibly divergent technology use patterns and expectations (2001a).

Throughout these chapters I use generational and age-based terminology. I do so not as an endorsement of the soundness of generational analysis, but in recognition that it is a central aspect of the discourse surrounding technology, learning, and libraries. The youngest cohort has many descriptors, including Generation Y, the Internet Generation, Generation Now, Generation Digital, Digital Natives, Generation Next, the Net Generation, the Google Generation, and/or Millennials. Older cohorts are described more simply and consistently as Generation X and Baby Boomers, a discrepancy that illustrates the degree to which a fixation on generational distinctions has become thematic in discussions of the "digital transition" (Joint Information Systems Committee [JISC], & the Centre for Information Behaviour and the Evaluation of Research [CIBER], 2008). Whenever possible I use neutral terms, or those that correspond with the language invoked by the authors or reports in question. Because a central goal of this project was to examine the generational speculation that tends to inform library technology development, in Part Two I compare and present findings using one of the best-known age/technology dichotomies, Prensky's digital natives and immigrants, against the less value-laden but still age-associated distinction between academic standing (graduate/undergraduate). Again, I compare these to test common academic, library, and technology assumptions as well as to investigate the strength of the association between age and academic standing.

Scope Note: Visible vs. Transparent Library Technologies

Because of its practical focus, the OU study did not analyze student receptivity to every conceivable application of Library 2.0. We were most interested in what can be best described as *visible* library technologies, or internet-based reference and access services delivered via commonly known and socially disruptive tools (e.g. text messaging, IM, customizable web browsers). These tend to require students to intentionally adopt, join, or integrate a library presence into more personal aspects of their technological milieux. Some visible technologies involve user agency to establish library contact at the point of need (e.g. Skyping a librarian, texting a call number), whereas others require students to opt in or subscribe to some form of library-initiated contact (e.g., RSS feeds, SMS alerts).

While the OU scanning project tracked student information, communication, and academic technologies as comprehensively as possible, the library technologies it investigated were included for their potential in a visible service context. We tracked student library technology receptivity to mobile internet use, social sites, web calling, browser customization, learning management system (LMS) integration, and text messaging. We also investigated student use, ownership, and perceptions of a number of personal and academic technologies already in use in the libraries, such as IM, blogs, wikis, and podcasts. Information and communication tools with a longer adoption trajectory or less local applicability in a direct service context were also included (e.g. Twitter, Second Life, gaming). Many specific technologies were selected for their relative popularity and/or brand-based ability to represent similar products (e.g., Meebo for web-based IM).

Not investigated by this report are the more *transparent* library technologies, or those that "seamlessly" integrate into the behind-the-scenes functionality of a library website or organization (Blyberg, 2008, para. 4). Transparent tools are less perceptible as library adaptations of personal platforms, such as open-source/social catalogs as well as some wikis and knowledgebases. These may be less identifiable as discrete 2.0 "technologies" when viewed from a library website (e.g., Library a la Carte, SOPAC, etc). Also included in this category are facility-based and instruction tools (e.g. roving librarians, classroom response systems). Due to their incorporeal and context-specific nature, effectively assessing transparent technologies in survey research is difficult. Qualitative, observational, and experimental research methods may be more appropriate means of evaluation.

The line separating visible and transparent library technologies is easily blurred. What constitutes transparency or visibility is relative depending on user perceptions - for some, the social and dynamic web has been and integral aspect of the entirety of their online experience. For others, blogs, texting, and other emerging technologies are still recognizable as novel. Chapters 4-6 report broad student library and technology use trends at Ohio University, but Chapter 7 focuses primarily on student receptivity to services that require purposeful use of personal and academic technologies to establish library contact and/or access information (e.g. Blackboard library chat, Firefox search toolbar). In contrast, online or facility-based services that use emerging technologies to enable less intentional, just-in-time assistance (e.g. Skype video kiosks, catalog tag clouds) are not examined in depth. Despite its focus on visible library technologies, the findings of this report carry significant implications for the evaluation and potential success of transparent library technologies in direct patron services, as well. Understanding student use, ownership, and/or familiarity with the fullest possible range of applications and concepts is critical to judging their potential scalability as library services.

Part I: Local Insight to Library Practice

Chapter 1: Change and Response

Librarians find ourselves at the heart of a debate over the evolving needs of an increasingly technocentric information culture. Perceived downward trends in readership and growing rates of online literacy lead some to predict the decline of traditional knowledge organizations, which struggle to adjust to the "digital transition" and its effect on user expectations, perceptions, and behaviors (Joint Information Systems Committee [JISC], & the Centre for Information Behaviour and the Evaluation of Research [CIBER], 2008). Others see opportunity in the changing landscape, championing expanded roles for libraries in areas such as digital information storage, access, protection, and advocacy. What is certain is that college and university librarians are continuously challenged to understand the dynamic information needs of incoming students, each cohort ostensibly clearer in its penchant for digital media, mobile and social technologies, ubiquitous internet access, collaborative and multitasked learning, and technology integration in the classroom (D. G. Oblinger & J. L. Oblinger, 2005).

From X to Millennial to Google to Y, a perceived generational shift in technology use and information-seeking behavior is widely discussed among theorists and demographers. Marc Prensky was among the first to distinguish a clear break in the abilities, perceptions, and attitudes of "digital natives," individuals born during or after the early 1980s who have never known life without pervasive connectivity (Prensky, 2001a, 2001b). More recently, others have resisted generational arguments as tokenizing and overly simplistic analyses of the broader social consequences of technology diffusion (Jenkins, 2007, Vaidhyanathan, 2008). The debate raises fundamental questions about the changing nature of literacy, and what role higher education should play in inculcating the skills and abilities necessary for students to thrive in the modern workforce (Jenkins, et al., 2006, EIU, 2008).

Whether real or imagined, the idea of a progressively digital student base has become a powerful change agent in academic libraries. The characterization of younger users as increasingly web-dependent puts them at variance with the prevailing perception of libraries as traditional, print-based institutions. This persistent "branding" is often invoked to explain declines in the library "mindshare," particularly among younger users (DeRosa, et al., 2006). College and university librarians are consequently reinvisioning technology, architecture, instruction, access, and public services for a new model of patron. These efforts reflect an ongoing and self-conscious digital transition within the field, facilitated in the past several years by the proliferation of mobile communication devices, Web 2.0 applications, and free/open source software.

The characteristic adaptability of these formats allows librarians and other educators to bypass the technological glass ceiling that previously separated programmer from user. Those without formal information technology skills are now increasingly able to contribute to a shifting educational landscape. As a result, calls to integrate emerging social and mobile tools in higher education are now common in the literature of instructional theory, curriculum design, and information studies.

From Web 2.0 to Library 2.0

As the market-driven movement towards a more participatory internet emerged, a related trend developed in the library world beginning in mid-2005. In what is best described as a widespread professional movement, "Library 2.0" has fostered extensive experimentation with dynamic content, mobile devices, and social tools for user services and professional development. In academic libraries, Library 2.0 quickly became the inspiration for a diverse range of programming as well as a rhetorical touchstone from which many have advocated for more interactive, responsive, and intuitive physical and digital spaces. The 2.0 approach has been compared to the *long tail* economic phenomenon in that it "[takes] the library to the user [and caters] to niche markets to fulfill unique user needs" (Griffis, et al., 2008, p. 1). Brian Kelley describes the movement as consisting of both *concepts,* such as "Openness" and "Trust Your User," and *tools* such as social sharing services, mashups, and virtual worlds (2008, p. 22). Early proponents of participatory library services encouraged a prototyping mentality more tolerant of the adaptable development model known as "constant beta." Many argue that these attitudes have inspired a necessary wave of experimentation in change-wary academic libraries.

Numerous services continue to be created or recast under the aegis of Library 2.0 and its ideal of more "user-centered" organizations. The most recognizable of its applications – RSS feeds, IM reference, podcasts, wikis, social catalogs, etc. – have spread throughout the profession virally via blogs, word of mouth, and skill-building programs such as Learning 2.0 (plcmcl2-about.blogspot.com/) and Five Weeks to a Social Library (www.sociallibraries.com/course/). In its professional communities of interest and practice, a do-it-yourself mentality has long been a feature of this movement. Librarians frequently rely on the accounts and advice of other practitioners during planning stages of emerging technology services, and an ethic of technological peer- and self-education has come to shape how many of us adopt social software, virtual communities, and mobile devices.

In pursuit of services based in emerging tools, many have discovered that one size unfortunately does not fit all where library innovation is concerned. Technology successes fail to translate neatly between institutions, meaning that one library's well-used chat widget can unintentionally become another's staffing nightmare. Long the subject of debate in the library blogosphere, scholarly research is beginning to confirm that similar mobile, social, and dynamic service models produce varied results in different settings (Naylor, Stoffel, and Van Der Laan, 2008; Booth, 2008, Blyberg, 2008). An overreliance on comparative benchmarking and a growing sense of technological peer pressure inspired the familiar cycle of 2.0 "bandwagon jumping", often criticized by Library 2.0's detractors as the librarian's equivalent of keeping up with the Jones'. Causes of this textbook-variety technolust are varied. To borrow Michael Stephens' phrasing - *technoenvy* (the sense that local services pale in comparison to peers) and *technopanic* (the feeling that users will jump ship if library sites, buildings, and services are not brought up to date, fast).

Rushing towards 2.0, many institutions bypassed local needs assessments and developed new products largely on generational assumptions of changing student information and technology expectations. Despite initial optimism, several years after the first wave of technology adoption many dynamic and social tools now (at best) languish quietly within library websites and social networking utilities, or (at worst) become high-profile failures that inspire outright skepticism on the part of library staff and/or patrons. This is increasingly apparent in the library blogosphere, where Library 2.0 has transitioned from an almost reverently praised movement to something akin to a cause célèbre. Some openly mock the enthusiasm of early "twopointopians", and many of Library 2.0's strongest proponents now argue for a more critical focus on the relevance and efficacy of library technology services in general (Annoyed Librarian, 2007, Blyberg, 2008, Farkas, 2008).

During a presentation with my former OU colleague Chris Guder at the 2009 ACRL conference, I asked a room of over 500 librarians how many of them could identify at least one Library 2.0 service at their local institutions. Almost every hand in the audience went up. When I asked the audience to keep their hands raised if this service had performed as well as they had hoped, every hand dropped - few even hesitated. Why have expectations so far exceeded results? It is my belief that many underperforming social and mobile library programs suffer from a lack of local insight during their planning and implementation phases. Compounded by complex hierarchical organizations that often restrict the "prototyping mentality" that can mitigate unanticipated (and inevitable) issues that accompany innovation, this has rendered many well-intentioned social, mobile, and/or dynamic library programs underused and/or overlooked.

Identical technologies give rise to distinct library services for the simple reason that local users and institutions are fundamentally unique. The reality of the matter is that unless the technology, information, and library facility needs and interests of users are locally examined and understood, librarians working with 2.0 technologies risk arbitrarily introducing hard-wrought innovations both to uninterested patrons and prohibitively unaccommodating workplaces. Rather than assuming that every library needs a blog, a wiki, and a podcast series, librarians who develop social and/or dynamic services should preface their efforts with local research in order to create a clearer perception of *actual*, rather than *imagined*, library and information needs of their immediate campus microcosm. Every institution must investigate the factors that shape its own landscape.

Local Cultures and Technology Adoption

The research process can tax resources and expertise, a reality that increases the temptation to draw heavily on external information sources for insight into local needs and expectations. In an attempt to "know their users," many have drawn largely on data gleaned from national studies, generational technology archetypes, and the experiences of peer institutions. In so doing, they inadvertently neglect to consider immediate user communities as well as the limitations and characteristics of their organizational cultures, leading in effect to emerging technology services tailored to other climates and therefore not well integrated, functional, or discoverable.

Technology is only one aspect of the overall effectiveness of a given library, and it is important to develop *holistic* tech-based services that work in tandem with, rather than apart from, other areas of an organization's impact. Because the potential ripple effects of Library 2.0 underperformance are significant, academic libraries must begin by asking, *"Can we use emerging information and communication technologies to increase our impact, and if so which tools are the most promising? How willing are users to integrate social and mobile library tools into their personal learning environments? First and foremost, how can we accurately and efficiently explore these questions?"*

Consider a recent study in which two universities in North Carolina replicated the 2005 OCLC *College Students' Perceptions of Libraries and Information Resources* survey, research that has had lasting impact on the field's understanding of student perceptions of the library "brand" (OCLC, 2005). Sutton and Bazirjian (2009) report that for each of the five open-ended OCLC survey questions replicated at their campuses (e.g., *What do you feel is the main purpose of a library? What is the first thing that you think of when you think of a library?*), not only were responses strikingly different from the original findings (which might reasonably be expected within a five-year gap), they also diverged widely between campuses based on demographic characteristics as well as institutional factors such as the physical condition of library facilities. The authors conclude that because the OCLC *Perceptions* findings are not representative of students at their or other campuses, "local data should be used for local decisions" (p. 189). My own research confirms that age-based generalizations and national survey data obscure the subtle specificity of distinct user communities.

Technology: Panacea or Pariah?

Many academic librarians share the conviction that the user relationship to information, communication technology, and literacy is in a state of flux. Redefining spaces and services in response to this change remains one of our most persistent challenges. What remains unclear is the degree to which the development cycle of Library 2.0 mobilizes an effective response on both macro and micro levels. The movement's strongest proponents encourage experimentation with collaborative and dynamic technologies in order to "meet users where they are" (Pin, 2007, p. 2). Alternatively, critics argue that this can result in the creation of "creepy treehouses," unwanted social library services that do more to alienate than to assist (Fister, 2008).

Despite our almost symbiotic reliance on computing, communication, and information tools, the effect of technology on libraries can be read as equal parts panacea and pariah. New platforms continue to transform operations and interactions, yet they also redefine cultural perceptions of libraries from without. Enhanced library computing facilities and learning/information commons are revitalizing library spaces, but search engines are routinely blamed for the declining use of library resources in student research. This tension has given rise to institutional responses to technology change that range from liberal to conservative, often within the same system or campus. One branch might welcome mobile phones and application downloading on library computers, whereas another might expressly forbid both. This creates a jarring experience for the user, who should expect to find a reasonably predictable and clearly communicated technology climate throughout an organization.

Hindsight and Library 2.0

Several years into the movement's development, hindsight has entered the Library 2.0 conversation in earnest. In its early days, advocates focused almost entirely on the transformational *promise* of social and collaborative library technologies. Emerging tools simply had not existed long enough or been widely enough adopted to be evaluated on a meaningful scale. During the 2.0 heyday, well-meaning and understandable enthusiasm led many early adopters to downplay the more sobering realities of creating, recreating, maintaining and modifying new user technologies. A rising complaint at conferences and among library bloggers has been that new services are not presented in a way that addresses the difficulties or practical outcomes of social technologies in a library setting. Emily Drabinski describes this frustration in *Library Praxis*: "there's always this persistent lack of data showing me that any of these things work. Sure, I know the stats about how many people are gaming and how many people are occupying virtual worlds, but I don't see any data that convinces me that people are playing *library* games, or occupying virtual *library* worlds" (2008). My own experience presenting on OU's groundbreaking but problematic "Skype a Librarian" pilots leads me to believe that Emily's complaint is typical. Few feel they are getting an accurate picture of how Library 2.0 services deliver, or what it takes to address problems when they arise. Attendees have thanked me for simply offering a critical perspective on the Skype pilots, addressing staffing and technology issues, explaining how we reconfigured services to address specific problems, and in particular for poking fun at our unanticipated blunders (Figure 1.1).

One explanation for the rose-colored glasses of early adopters (myself included among them) lies in the fact that those promoting mobile, social, and user-created library content simply did not know how these tools would play out, only that they had the potential to redefine the library paradigm. Social library services were frequently promoted as universally useful, and often misinterpreted as universally necessary. In practice, this often resulted in an approximation of the following vicious cycle: a technologically savvy librarian with strong administrative support and experimental leeway at one institution creates a pilot program using a relatively far-flung tool, actively testing an "if you build it, they will come" service philosophy. A number of relatively inexperienced but highly motivated librarians at other institutions read about this service on the first librarian's blog, rushing to duplicate it without local research or adequate knowledge of the technology's potential flaws, only to be frustrated by low use and/or performance. Two years later, a librarian in a technology-negative organizational climate considers developing the now much more widely established library technology locally. Upon finding several less-than-successful iterations of the original service on other library sites, s/he decides that the potential local fallout from a failed venture is prohibitive.

Figure 1.1 A Patron Taunts the Skype Kiosk

In this scenario, the viral nature of Library 2.0 actually precludes the development of used and useful library services. This is due to a) lack of communication by the initial innovator regarding potential technical caveats and the success-enabling characteristics of their local institution, b) inadequate needs assessment and service customization by the second group of developers, and c) excessive negativity caused by a hostile technology environment and a consequent inability to anticipate success by the third adopter. Each party should have grounded their efforts in a clearer foundation of actual user needs and potential technology applications in a local setting, instead finding themselves thwarted by an excessive focus on peer expectations and experiences.

Demographics and User Profiling

At most academic libraries, the adoption of a user-focused service philosophy results in an array of products with social, mobile, and dynamic characteristics. Tag-enabled catalogs, custom search toolbars, library blogs, IM or widget-based reference, subject and staff wikis, and so forth are combined, hacked, and overlapped by early adopters who tend to "bring along" their colleagues by degree. To inform how they choose and shape new services, these librarians often attempt to anticipate the information needs of the different patron communities they serve (e.g. undergraduates, faculty, graduate students) and respond to these needs via homegrown configurations of tech-based and traditional programming. The perception that an underperforming local service can be enhanced by a specific social or mobile technology often inspires this process. Library 2.0 became popular in part for its ability to enable creative, free and/or open source solutions to persistent problems.

Library 2.0 has inspired academic librarians to systematically investigate emerging mobile and participatory web technologies for their potential to provide access to information in innovative ways. Sensing that libraries would become irrelevant if they did not respond to changing user technologies, early adopters first carved out a niche using instant messaging (IM) and social sites, gradually coming to test the gamut of new tools. A common expectation of the Library 2.0 approach has been that social, dynamic, and mobile products, formats, and environments can be tailored to fit the needs different kinds of library users. Similarly, a fundamental assumption of user-centered library technology development is that users will adopt emerging services that mirror their communication and productivity preferences. In effect, much of the library "long tail" consists of *personal* 2.0 technologies that have been transformed into *library* 2.0 technologies.

Emerging library services are often intended to increase the library profile at different "points of need." Determining what constitutes a point of need involves connecting technology types with target audiences. Each audience is thought to use new tools in ways that correspond with the demographic characteristics that shape their relationship to learning, libraries, and information. Services are therefore often developed for and promoted to specific library audiences, e.g., social networking groups, applications, and/or profiles for undergraduates, browser add-ons or library toolbars for faculty and graduate students. To an extent, this process reflects the technique of consumer profiling commonly employed by advertisers, the difference being that in libraries decisions are not grounded in detailed market research. The same can be said for other areas of library operations – often, conjecture informs everything from facility hours to access policies.

Librarians pursue new tools in hopes of appealing to the demographic characteristics, expectations, and interests of distinct patron archetypes that naturally emerge from academia's disciplines, statuses, and age cohorts. In essence, Library 2.0 technologizes long-identified core library user groups. Emerging technology markets are usually defined by a generational formula that associates aptitude and affiliation with information need: because (Millennials, Boomers, Generation X) use *personal* technology A, they will want to use *library* technology B. Undergraduates correspond with the Google Generation or Generation Y, commonly viewed as technology fluent and hyperconnected. Faculty and returning students (Baby Boomers) are seen as more sporadic technology users, somewhat less likely to adopt 2.0 tools. Graduate students (Generation X) are technological wildcards swayed by the needs of their discipline.

From Assumption to Inference

While technology aptitudes and information seeking traits may be broadly shared among college and university students and/or faculty, the organizational structures and cultural milieux of the institutions that enroll, employ, and educate them are instrumental in influencing how individuals shape their own "personal learning environments," and consequently the extent to which they involve the library in this process. Academic institutions reflect the social system of privilege and prestige that grants individuals access to education and technology, meaning that each institution has a unique demographic personality composed of many subcultures. By extension, each campus develops a distinct library culture, influenced by many factors, ranging from physical (library architecture, availability of campus student centers) to demographic (average student age, proportion of distance learners) to cultural (library awareness, income level, nationality, academic motivation) and so forth.

In an ongoing effort to create effective and engaging libraries, using data to move from assumption to inference discourages the more speculative impulses that arise from the unlimited customization potential of new web and communication tools. It is incumbent upon academic librarians to develop strategies to investigate our own contexts in order to work from an informed perception of the communities we serve. Locally developed research can reveal if there is a disconnect between desired levels of information access and delivery, and in a more creative, informative, and customizable manner than is often possible using externally created survey instruments. The Ohio University Libraries conducted a customized local environmental scan in an attempt to understand how and why our students were actually using libraries and technology, instead of how we (or other researchers) hoped and/or feared they were. Studying our students eased the commonly held sense of technology pressure, created an accessible feedback record that shed light on usage statistics, and facilitated patron-focused change throughout the entire organization. Our experience demonstrates that homegrown user assessment need not be prohibitively complex in order to evaluate and prioritize library technology and beyond.

Chapter 2: Literature Review

Many library decisions are based on assumptions about patron expectations, and generational arguments have strengthened our collective conviction that user relationships to libraries and technology are changing in age-predictable ways. Research consistently indicates that younger respondents tend to own more mobile tools and use more social sites than ever before. However, this does not necessarily translate to a viable audience for library tools built on these platforms, nor does it reflect the composition or needs of a given campus. In the previous chapter I argued that in order to be more truly user-focused, librarians should challenge demographic assumptions and leverage locally developed assessments to get to the core of how students understand libraries and technology. Becoming conversant with national research is a critical step in this process, as it creates an important foundation upon which to pursue local investigations. The following review of literature provides baseline understanding of generational aspects of technology use, the response of higher education to technology change, and student perspectives on libraries, technology, and information.

Generations in Transition

Many theorists describe changes in the technology, media, information, and learning behaviors of successive generations. While there is little consensus on nomenclature, age demarcations, or the value of generational analysis itself, a considerable body of work has emerged arguing that age cohorts are distinct in the ways they use and relate to technology. Mark Presnky's *digital native* and *digital immigrant* typography is among the earliest and most widely known perspectives on the defining characteristics of those who matured before and after the advent of internet saturation (2001a, 2001b). According to Prensky, digital immigrants (born prior to the early 1980s) interact with technology on a heightened learning curve and view emerging tools as novelties, whereas digital natives (born during or after the early 1980s) have come of age immersed in the information and communication technology-rich environment and are thought to be more comfortable with existing in a state of constant "beta."

Prensky describes cognitive changes caused by lifelong technology immersion, stating that digital natives tend to "think and process information fundamentally differently than their predecessors" (2001a, p. 1). Some believe that the concept of technology itself has changed for younger learners (D. G. Oblinger & J. L. Oblinger, 2005). Jukes (2007) posits that recent generations are so comfortable in the digital world that they consider it comprised of tools and processes rather than technologies, which motivates them to "use technology transparently, without marveling at it" (p. 4). Lippincott (2007) argues that, in addition to learning and thinking differently than previous cohorts,

Millennials tend to consider themselves active "content creators" rather than passive information consumers (p. 16). Her argument is supported by *Living and Learning with New Media: Summary of Findings of the Digital Youth Project,* a recent MacArthur Foundation report on media, technology, and learning in the information age (Ito, et al., 2009).

As a negative corollary to their apparent multitasking abilities, youth are often characterized as possessing decreased information discovery and evaluation abilities. Prensky (2001b) cites findings indicating that the diffracted attention patterns exhibited by digital natives negatively impacts their ability for *reflection*, the process that enables critical thinking and the construction of "mental models" (p. 5). More youth now rely on non-library information sources during their college and university years when the need for peer-reviewed research is high, suggesting a leveling effect in student perceptions of information quality. That incoming cohorts consider web-based information to be easier to use than library-based information has been widely documented (JISC & CIBER, 2008).

Despite the prevalence of generational technology analysis, a recent Joint Information Systems Committee & Centre for Information Behaviour and the Evaluation of Research study, *Information Behaviour of the Researcher of the Future*, questions whether the newest cohort of learners is as "qualitatively 'different' than what went before" as many assume (2008, p. 18). This exhaustively researched longitudinal study of library, education, and information studies literature suggests that a number of common assumptions regarding the "Google Generation" are misguided. A principal claim disputed by the study is that immersive web searching makes today's youth somehow more expert at rapid information acquisition. Other "myths" called into question include whether digital natives are actually trial and error learners, inherently skilled multitaskers, and/or more impatient with information delay than older generations. The study also examines whether youth give friends and family undue credibility as information sources, and even if they are as internet-engaged as often portrayed.

Information Behaviour of the Researcher of the Future cautions readers against "neat generational labeling" of youth technology culture (p. 21) The JISC/CIBER findings suggest that many traits often associated with "digital youth" have been based more on conjecture than research. The report suggests that instead of being confined to a certain age range, technology aptitudes are likely diffusing at different rates throughout society as a consequence of widespread web, mobile and computing saturation (p. 21). The degree of technology facility in a given individual is determined by a variety of demographic factors such as age, income, and educational attainment. The acquisition of these skills may simply be more dramatic among the young, making it easy to overlook common social shifts that are simply less apparent or anticipated in older generations. Ascribing vast digital strides to younger generations likely reflects some measure of technology anxiety on the part of their predecessors, who may feel that innovation occurs too rapidly to manageably "keep up".

Cultural theorist and professor of information technology Siva Vaidhyanathan flatly asserts, "there is no such thing as the 'digital generation'" (2008, para. 1). Attesting first-hand to the disparate abilities of undergraduate students, he cautions against the temptation to imagine common technology skills across broad swaths of the population. Vaidhyanathan argues that generational claims disregard the diverse and income-imbalanced technological landscape within higher education, and are even less accurate when applied to society at large. He argues that being "born digital" is a more a mark of economic and social privilege than generational allegiance. In a 2007 blog post titled "Reconsidering Digital Immigrants," prominent media theorist Henry Jenkins writes that age-based generalizations "impl[y] that there is a world which these people all share and a body of knowledge they have all mastered, rather than seeing the online world as unfamiliar and uncertain for all of us" (Jenkins, 2008, para. 7). Not only does the idea of a digital "native" obscure the range of technological access, skills, and comfort levels among youth, it has the effect of portraying older cohorts as uniformly inept. Jenkins goes so far as to compare this aspect of Prensky's native/immigrant dichotomy to jingoist portrayals of cultural outsiders, arguing that it negates the contributions of generational diversity to the information landscape. In effect, "digital immigrants compute with an accent: they talk funny." (para. 13).

Jenkins, Vaidhyanathan, and the group of researchers that produced *Living and Learning with New Media: Summary of Findings of the Digital Youth Project* encourage more nuanced attention to the individual, creative, and participatory experiences that youth fashion through technology (Ito, et al., 2009). They argue that technology can be an empowering vehicle for individual expression, but that it is by no means uniformly used or even widely available to all young people. These authors, who I characterize as generational realists, reject technological utopianism and affirm the importance of customization in the way young people relate to emerging tools and applications. Like librarians who have taken several steps back from the heady promise of Library 2.0, these authors question the idea of "digital youth" itself. Instead, they encourage us to consider technology as part of the way all create customized personal environments for learning and play. The 2009 *Horizon Report* predicts that the concept of a multidimensional "personal web" is one of the technology trends that will most affect higher education in the coming several years (Johnson, Levine, & Smith, 2009). The personal web is a way of shaping the online environment so that it "explicitly supports one's social, professional, learning, and other activities" (Johnson, Levine, & Smith, 2009, p. 4). The user desire to configure free, easy-to-use widgets, browser extensions, and applications according to their own needs can inform how academic librarians view not only technology development, but buildings and traditional patron services. Virtual as well as physical library spaces should help users to customize their ideal learning and research experiences.

Student Technology Use and Ownership

Despite recent challenges to generational technology assumptions, a large body of survey research demonstrates clear connections between age and technology use, consumption, and perceptions. The Pew/Internet and American Life Project's 2007 *Typology of Information and Communication Technology Users* demonstrates the tendency of younger people to not only own and use more technology, but to be more positively disposed towards innovation itself. Technological "omnivores," or respondents with a "richly participatory relationship with digital content and a strong sense that information and communication technology makes life easier," were the youngest (median age 28) and most technologically inclined of all respondents (Horrigan, 2007, p. 6). Omnivores typically considered themselves early technology adopters and were likely to own and use a range of innovative tools and gadgets. Although younger respondents were dispersed throughout the remaining nine categories of "low, medium, and elite" technology use, increased age was directly proportional to decreased use and less favorable disposition towards various types of media and technology.

The annual *ECAR Study of Undergraduate Students and Information Technology* tracks student ownership and perceptions of information, communication, and academic technologies at over 100 North American campuses. Their 2004-2008 reports confirm many of the Pew *Typology* findings in a higher education context. Longitudinal data reveal an increasing tendency among undergraduates to own mobile devices such as laptop computers, cellular phones, and portable audio players (Caruso & Salaway, 2008). Younger respondents also tended to use social software, IM, and other emerging technologies at greater rates than older students, and were more likely to view themselves as early or mainstream technology adopters. Undergraduates in the 2007 survey rated themselves as relatively highly skilled in common computing and academic tasks, spent an average of 18 hours per week online, were connected via broadband or wireless access, and contrary to predictions still overwhelmingly used email for official and academic correspondence (Caruso & Salaway, 2007). Student reliance on email challenges the notion that more disruptive tools will outmode all "legacy" technologies.

The Demographic Divide

The gender, economic, and cultural differences revealed by numerous studies suggests that unless careful demographic analysis of survey research is conducted, findings can lead to a false perception of uniformity by obscuring deep disparities among respondents. Evidence indicates that even within the relatively privileged microcosm of higher education, there is considerable demographic variability in technology use, ownership, and skill. Age, gender, economic status, and major are categories within higher education representative of the well-known concept of the racial, geographic, and class-based cultural "digital divide" in technology use and ownership (Servon, 2002). Male-gendered and/or science and IT-oriented majors report higher technology ownership levels, adoption profiles, and confidence, whereas female-gendered and/or less economically privileged respondents tend to have lower self-perceptions of technical skill and ownership (Caruso, et al., 2006). In a study of technology "FITness" (Fluency with Information Technology) at Southwestern University, McEuen confirmed gender differences in student self-assessment of technology competency (2001). However, the inverse effect is evident in social software use. Lenhart (2007) has shown that among digital natives, teenage girls dominate socially oriented content creation, including blogging, photosharing, and participation in "online conversations."

Shifting Literacies

Ubiquitous connectivity and user-generated content culture has led theorists to describe a "convergence of literacies" spanning the textual, information, technology, and visual (Lippincott, 2007, p. 16). Lippincott (2007) argues that as new media, information, and social technologies become inextricably linked, it will be necessary for students in higher education to develop multiple literacies in order to be effective information consumers and producers. Jenkins, Clinton, Purushotma, Robison, & Weigel (2006) identify a set of core skills that will be required for students to thrive in what has become a digital "participatory culture," including *play, performance, simulation, appropriation, multitasking, distributed cognition, collective intelligence, judgment, transmedia navigation, networking,* and *negotiation* (pp. 3-4).

Significant cultural and pedagogical developments are occurring in higher education as the academy responds to actual or perceived shifting student literacies (Johnson, Levine, & Smith, 2009, 2008, 2007, 2006). The increasing prevalence of distance and collaborative learning programs, the changing nature of scholarly research, and heightened information delivery expectations are among the many factors motivating the trend towards technology integration by institutions of higher learning. While the diffusion of innovation through academe is a typically protracted process, recent *Horizon Reports* identify a number of technologies on the current "adoption horizon" that are already affecting classroom instruction and student learning behavior, such as social networking, user-created content, mobile devices, virtual worlds, educational gaming, and the "new scholarship" (Johnson, Levine, & Smith, 2007, p. 5). The 2008 and 2009 *Horizon* reports identify similar trends, adding mashups, social operating systems, grassroots video, cloud computing, and personal webs (Johnson, Levine, & Smith, 2008, 2009).

Technology Integration in Higher Education

As instructors gain greater comfort with technology, incoming students are increasingly satisfied with its pedagogical applications and have begun expect new platforms as an integral aspect of their coursework. The 2008 *ECAR* undergraduate study reports that from 2004-2008 students continued to find value in the expanding array of computing devices and skills in higher education, demonstrating growing satisfaction with new learning tools such as web based games, wikis, and blogs (Caruso & Salaway, 2008). Longitudinal data from ECAR indicates that learning management system (LMS) use in universities is steadily rising, and that students are "overwhelmingly positive" about the LMS as a learning platform (Caruso, et al., 2006, p. 6, Caruso & Salaway, 2008). Of particular relevance to academic librarians, undergraduates often cited convenience and research facilitation as the greatest benefits of technology in their academic lives (Caruso, et al., 2006).

This emerging IT consciousness in higher education is far from uncritical. Learners perceive that poorly executed technology hinders educational experiences, and they expect technical proficiency from their instructors. Some students express the desire for technical training in areas in which they may be inexpert (Caruso & Salaway, 2007). Students tend to prefer judicious rather than extensive use of course-based IT, and still highly value face-to-face interaction with instructors (Caruso & Salaway, 2008). Researchers at the Digital Media Center at The University of Minnesota conducted a study of its Twin Cities students, finding that respondents had generally positive attitudes towards the "constructive" use of classroom and LMS technologies (Walker & Jorn, 2007). The most recent ECAR survey also reports a leveling effect in age-based preferences for technology integration (Caruso & Salaway, 2008). Contrary to previous years when younger students actually indicated a preference for *less* technology in their classes, the 2008 survey saw similarly moderate enthusiasm among all respondents. The authors postulate, "technology is becoming increasingly integrated into the lives of students at all ages" (Caruso & Salaway, 2008, p. 11).

Student technical skill self-assessment is similarly complex. In the ECAR studies, students between 2004 and 2008 tended to rate themselves highly in common academic and computing tasks such as LMS use, presentation creation, and word processing. High technology self-assessment in these areas did not extend to more advanced activities such as multimedia production and web editing, however. Instead of being universally skilled in higher-order technological pursuits such as coding and graphic design, students consistently reported lower abilities in these and other advanced computing applications, even when they also perceived themselves as early technology adopters (Caruso & Salaway, 2008). Vaidhyanathan states that in a decade of observing university students few have demonstrated this depth of technical expertise, indicating that facility with internet, media, and social applications does not translate to higher-order technology skills (2008).

Library Use and Perceptions

The American Library Association reports that public library use increased dramatically between 1994 and 2004 at a rate of 61% (cited in Vaidhyanathan, 2008.) Despite less than favorable overall perceptions of libraries, the OCLC survey project *College Students' Perceptions of Libraries and Information Resources* finds that college and university students are even more frequent library users than the general population, while future college students (14-17 year-olds) demonstrated the highest current and potential use of all respondents (DeRosa et al., 2006). While students report that their use of libraries has declined in proportion to the rise of the internet, the 2007 *ECAR Study of Undergraduate Students and Information Technology* found that over 95% of undergraduates use their university library on at least a monthly basis (Caruso & Salaway).

In spite of dramatic shifts in the service and access models of college and university libraries, much seems to have been lost on student users. Mass digitization, transitional literacies, and distance education are among many external factors that threaten to obscure the traditional library image among higher education students. Despite the fact that academic libraries have been among the strongest advocates for development in many digital areas, many learners still think of libraries as little more than print repositories (DeRosa, et al., 2006). A number of theories explain this persistent perceptual disconnect, such as our continued inability to make online resources more transparent and discoverable, lagging efforts to promote changing services to user populations, and lack of sufficient resources to compete with the pace of commercial information and technology development. Students remain largely unfamiliar with the range of digital resources that have been vastly expanded over the last decade, and are particularly uninformed about the existence of digitized books (DeRosa et al., 2006, *Wired Campus Newsletter*, 2008).

The OCLC report also finds that search engines tend to better mesh with student expectations of information accessibility, and are typically rated equally trustworthy as library-based information. That said, OCLC reports that higher education students are more likely to state that libraries are about "information" than non-student respondents. This indicates that to some degree the perspective of libraries as warehouses of printed material may be changing (DeRosa, et al., 2006). The ongoing "Library as Place" movement that has advocated creating more community-based physical spaces for students is likely one factor in this evolving perspective (Council on Library and Information Resources, 2005).

Local User Research: Creating Context

A number of recent surveys and field studies at college and university libraries illustrate the insight that can be gained by establishing stronger local cultures of assessment. In an innovative ethnographic project at the University of Rochester, Foster and Gibbons (2007) explored the undergraduate research process. Their findings highlight students' "self-service" orientation, a desire for 24/7 remote access, and their sometimes-erroneous perceptions of academic libraries. The authors note that "students tend to be overly confident of their self-service skills in the library arena," and when frustrated in an information search, often "[assume] that the library simply does not have the resources" instead of persisting or seeking assistance (p. 77).

The 21st Century Library Project: Designing a Research Library of the Future for New York University explored the digital and physical research needs of graduate students and faculty (2007). A series of focus groups revealed a graduate student population dependent on digital resources, generally unsatisfied with library research platforms, and unsure of their own abilities to use or seek help with information tools. Participants wanted libraries to function better not only as information repositories, but also as learning communities or "thought centers." They also identified the ascendancy of new communication methods and media in scholarship, and discussed the potential role of the library in their development of pedagogical and collaboration skills. A comparable project at the University of Minnesota reports similar sentiments among graduate students, who demonstrated a preference for digital content and emphasized the need for more usable libraries overall (Marcus, et al., 2007).

Each of these projects exemplifies how local investigation can contextualize the baseline of understanding provided by external technology and library assessment initiatives. In each case, local information was applied towards programmatic ends - evaluating, modifying, and developing services based on actual feedback. The Rochester, New York University, and Minnesota initiatives were all comprehensive, but research does not necessarily need to be conducted on this large a scale to be effective. There are many approaches to user assessment, all of which can increase working knowledge of user populations, library satisfaction, and the potential reception of technology-based library products. Focus groups, usability studies, polls, interviews, direct observation, and questionnaires can be combined in a number of ways based on contextual needs and resources. Extant local knowledge of user populations and library goals allows homegrown studies to illuminate contextual nuance and character, customization that can be difficult to achieve when using externally developed survey instruments. In the following chapter, I discuss the Ohio University Student Technology Survey in order to provide insight into the practical or "action" research process. I outline considerations important in developing and deploying local studies, focusing in particular on web-based surveys as one of the most accessible and cost-effective research methods.

Chapter 3: Homegrown Research – Design, Implementation, and Analysis

Now more than ever, academic libraries are challenged to devise strategies that help them respond to changing user needs and financially strained institutional climates (Deiss & Petrowski, 2009). Often invoked as a corollary to Library 2.0, many have advocated for the establishment of library "cultures of assessment," in which data and research informs decision-making and development. Lakos (2007) argues that due to mounting external challenges, a growing need to demonstrate library value within academia, and the ultimate accountability we have to users, assessment of all kinds should be integrally woven throughout library organizations. By establishing a more "results-oriented perspective," the past model of internally focused, conjecture-based operations can be reversed and greater attention paid to patron expectations (Lakos, 2007, p. 432). While many are already tacitly assessment-oriented, Lakos observes that "libraries, in general, recognize the value of collecting and using data for planning and decision-making, but they do not do this systematically or effectively" (2007, p. 431). One or two librarians developing surveys in isolation do not create cultures of assessment. Reflective investigation has to be encouraged at all levels of an organization (Lakos, 2007, Lakos & Phipps, 2004). The library that supports an inquiry-based *learning culture* will be more able perceive and shape its impact on the community it serves.

Many types of evaluation can facilitate more reflective library cultures. The spectrum of research activity ranges from *basic*, *pure*, or *fundamental* studies intended to inform core principles of human knowledge, to *practical* or *applied* assessment that influences actionable ends. Studies from across the spectrum can be *nonexperimental* or *experimental*, either objectively observing phenomena or shaping conditions in order to understand their effects. The vast majority of library research is practical, observational, descriptive, and nonexperimental in character, and is conducted to varying degrees of intensity based on local needs, buy-in, and resources. There are countless motivations for conducting assessment in an academic library setting, such as the desire to understand a particular audience, evaluate services, track changes in traffic, circulation, and acquisitions, gauge skills and abilities, and to appraise patron satisfaction.

This chapter is a case study in one institution's experience actualizing a culture of assessment through *user research*, an aspect of library evaluation that focuses on the needs and characteristics of potential and existing customers (as opposed to staff or operations). While opportunities for user research have always been abundant, methods for gathering input are increasingly accessible due to the participatory nature of many emerging technologies. User research can foster communication between a library, its patrons, and other campus stakeholders, helping to diffuse understanding and a sense of community ownership over a local library's current and future offerings. When tracked over time, collected data can portray changing expectations and inform the results-based decision making process crucial to library adaptation.

Although the OU environmental scan used web-based survey methodology, many of the insights I provide into the practicalities of conducting user research can be applied to other types of evaluation. Towards this end, I describe the OU project in detail while making broad observations that may prove useful in other contexts. Because the strength of local data is in its specificity, the experience of Ohio University should be viewed as a template rather than a model and adjusted accordingly in order to accommodate the working cultures of other organizations. The culture of the Alden Library Reference and Instruction Department was paramount in facilitating a productive assessment climate, allowing the project to develop and change organically instead of experiencing "death by committee." The flexibility of a team-based environment allowed me to move forward with the research both independently and collaboratively, requesting feedback and assistance when necessary. In addition, the OU Libraries' supportive environment prevented the sense of perfectionism that can so easily hinder progress in an institutional context.

Research is a challenging process best learned by doing. For this author, the OU Student Technology Survey was a veritable crash-course in applied assessment that required the acquisition of many unexpected skills in research design, survey construction, marketing, data analysis, and information presentation. This lengthy treatment of findings emerged from the unique opportunity I had to evaluate survey data from a number of perspectives. In addition to producing a local report for the Ohio University Libraries, I analyzed survey data in conjunction with the final project required of a MEd in Computer Education and Technology, a degree I pursued at the OU College of Education while working as a Reference/Instruction Librarian. Though this dual focus I was able to reflect at length on what is required for effective user research in formal as well as action-oriented contexts, and to the produce the correlation analyses in Chapters 4 and 7 that would otherwise have been outside the normal scope of practical, workplace research.

Research Scalability

Like Library 2.0, "culture of assessment" is easier to invoke than it is to realize. Fostering productive library evaluation cultures may be difficult for a variety of reasons - less-than-rigorous training in research methods in MLIS education and a lack of institutional support are common impediments. More important than the extent or character of library research is that it emerges from "a belief in the need for continuous learning," and ultimately succeeds in informing local action (Lakos & Phipps, 2004, p. 351). Not all assessment has to be intensive to be effective, and varying levels of rigor are appropriate for different applications. Statistical and sampling concerns such as confidence intervals, sample size, reliability, and so forth should not loom so large as to stymie local efforts, and data that will be used on the fly need not be held to the same standards as information that will be made widely available or published. Keeping this fundamental concept of *scalability* in mind can reduce the intimidation many experience when considering a research design. Despite the relative flexibility of practical library assessment, it is still important to take steps to ensure that the information you collect is sound and reliable, if not expressly "scientific."

Environmental Scanning

Environmental scans should take the library pulse of a campus, portraying not only demographics and statistics but also gestalt - the habits, desires, criticism, and praise that emerge from the individual relationships users form with libraries and technology. The OU project focused on students in order to tailor our investigations to their specific context and needs. If they succeed in casting a wide and representative net, environmental scans can help an institution leverage local insight to create a multifaceted response to user expectations. Current trends within libraries and higher education dictate that environmental scans of any kind gravitate towards a focus on technology and user expectations, which reduces the guesswork inherent in interpreting external data on a local level. Research that investigates both student and faculty library and technology perceptions should be a core component of any user assessment program. That said, while technology change is a key motivator for much library assessment activity, by no means should the scope of a research project be limited to emerging tools and their implications for service development.

The Association of College & Research Libraries (www.acrl.org/ala/mgrps/divs/acrl/publications/whitepapers/Environmental_Scan_2.pdf) and the Online Computer Library Center (www.oclc.org/us/en/reports/escan/default.htm) both conducted environmental scans within the last several years, producing reports that identify major social and technological developments affecting librarianship. Environmental scanning in large membership organizations such as ACRL and OCLC is a necessarily broad undertaking aimed at identifying macro-level trends. At individual libraries, environmental scans can also focus on cultural minutiae, charting specific user opinions, perceptions, and behaviors. In order to gather a representative sample, local scans will typically be collected via large-scale online surveys similar to the one described in this report. They can also be supplemented by or comprised of assessments of varied methodologies. When systematically developed, a series of smaller questionnaires, interviews, and focus groups can provide a wealth of cumulative insight.

Comprehensive national surveys such as OCLC's 2005 *College Students' Perceptions of Libraries and Information Resources* and the annual *ECAR Study of Undergraduate Students and Information Technology* can provide excellent methodological and topical inspiration for librarians conducting local assessments. The questionnaires used in the OU scan were heavily informed by OCLC and ECAR's publicly available survey instruments in both content and format. OCLC and ECAR findings also allowed us to broadly consider potential commonalities and differences in our students compared to a national baseline, although our intention was never to replicate these studies in order to benchmark findings. Rather, we wanted to gain specific understanding of our own student community in order to make service decisions that more authentically reflected their needs.

My research indicates that technology decisions based on assumptions informed by external data misrepresented our users by its lack of substantive understanding of their specific context and culture. This substance was gained by adding nuance to the somewhat characterless technology and library use data generated by our closed-form questions in Survey 1 (e.g., multiple choice, Likert scale) – a series of open-ended items in Survey 2 provided invaluable verbatim insight into student integration of library services into their overall academic experience. By combining multiple methods of assessment within our survey instruments, we were able to gauge how students appreciated, used, (mis)understood, and criticized "the library" and its extant and nascent services.

Institutional Research Climates

Librarians planning to conduct local scans should first gain insight into their campus and library research cultures, which can exert enormous influence on every step of the process. How an institution allows its constituents to be studied, incentivized, and communicated with is usually outlined in a series of policies and that can have bearing on the ultimate impact of study findings.

Offices of Institutional Research

Colleges and universities rely heavily on internal statistics for purposes of evaluation, benchmarking, and public relations, and common standards of operational transparency make a great deal of valuable information open to public review. Institutions that facilitate faculty research develop protocol for regulating surveys and studies of all kinds. They also invariably support local offices of institutional research that provide important sources of demographic information, advice, promotional opportunities, and potential collaboration for librarians.

Any academic librarian interested in "knowing their users" should consult the website of their campus office of institutional research and/or research compliance. At a minimum, departments of institutional research typically provide annual fact sheets containing information on student demographics, and will often publish and archive many other studies that examine and document campus life. Prior to designing a research instrument it is good practice to investigate any studies, surveys, and reports that are available, which will almost always feature information regarding various aspects of a campus' social and academic makeup. They can also illuminate the characteristics of sound research instruments and provide the statistical basis for determining whether a library study has gathered a representative sample of the student population.

Research Compliance

Offices of institutional research often contain institutional review boards (IRBs), also known as ethical review boards (ERBs) or independent ethics committees (IECs). These federally sanctioned panels monitor institutionally supported research to ensure that it is conducted safely and ethically. Institutional review is an important and often requisite aspect of research projects involving human subjects, which includes focus groups and survey research. If research compliance is required, it can extend the timeline of practical user assessment considerably. Institutional review may not be necessary, however, because many institutions grant exemptions for practical research that is primarily intended to inform or benefit the operations of a campus unit.

Institutions vary widely in the strictness of their requirements for submitting action or practical research projects for institutional review, and local offices of research compliance should be contacted to gain general insight into regulations and requirements. According to the protocol of the Ohio University Office of Research Compliance, because the Student Technology Survey project contributed directly to library operations and the identities of participants were kept private, IRB approval was deemed unnecessary. Conversely, in the University of Rochester *Studying Students* initiative, Foster and Gibbons report that their project was subjected to full IRB review, ostensibly due to external funding and the personal nature of some of their ethnographic methodologies (2007).

Institutional Study Participation

It is important to determine if your campus or library participates in institutional, consortial, or national studies that may have the potential to inform the way local research is conducted. For example, the well-known annual *ECAR Study of Undergraduates and Information Technology* is compiled from findings generated from over 100 North American colleges and research institutions. Ohio University is not an ECAR participant, and I therefore consulted their survey instrument for topical and organizational inspiration (net.educause.edu/ir/library/pdf/SI/ESI08a.pdf). The ECAR instrument covers student use and ownership of a variety of computing and communication technologies, as well as library use and information literacy self-assessments. Before conducting an environmental scan, consult the ECAR list of participants in order to avoid unnecessary duplication of effort (connect.educause.edu/Library/ECAR/TheECARStudyofUndergradua/47485). If your campus does participate in the survey, it may be possible to gain access to local results and/or a data set.

Libraries should also investigate assessment opportunities that exist via non-library venues, such as annual institutional surveys, the campus learning management system, social networking sites, or the university website. Depending on campus communication policies, it can be difficult to reach wide audiences via email or other methods in order to generate representative samples. Gaining access to a campus-wide survey conducted by departments such as information or educational technology can consequently be invaluable in expanding the reach of a research project. Adding library-oriented items to existing campus studies may mean that fewer subjects can be covered, but it can also build collaborative relationships and reach a larger sample population.

Developing a Local Research Project

A number of stages are important for conducting effective and reliable user research. In the following section, I describe in general terms the steps undertaken by myself and the Reference and

Instruction Technology Team during the design, administration, and reporting of the OU environmental scan. These are not concrete rules that need to be followed to the letter. Rather, they are observations that may prove useful to those designing similar assessments. Throughout this section, I describe the process involved in conducting research of a primarily practical nature, which produces data intended principally to inform local decisions rather than for publication. Because of my intention to conduct more advanced statistical analysis of the data produced by the OU Student Technology Survey, my research process was at times more rigorous than might be required of action-oriented contexts. Consequently, I address differently scaled approaches in order to highlight the flexibility of practical compared to formal research.

Scope and Purpose

The first step of any practical assessment is to determine a *scope* and *purpose*, or who you hope to investigate, what you want to understand about them, and why. Developing a scope and purpose can be a relatively informal process, but should have the effect of helping you create more productively focused instruments. *The OU environmental scan surveyed students in order to gain actionable insight into their library and technology cultures. Our research assessed a series of demographic assumptions that motivated the library's decision-making process in regards to emerging technology services.* This simple statement of scope and purpose illustrates that it should be possible to describe a project using concise statements that communicate a clear justification for the research. Complexity will naturally emerge as you form research questions, craft survey instruments, and perform data analysis.

Homegrown vs. Packaged Instruments

Developing a research project from the ground up is an intensive process, and it is sound practice to avoid reinventing the wheel whenever possible. One way to mitigate assessment redundancy is to consider the use of externally developed instruments. These outside assessments have the advantage of rigorous reliability and validity, aspects of sound design that increase confidence in the conclusions you are able to draw from collected data. They also increase the potential for what I think of as benchmarkability, or the opportunity to compare findings against peer institutions. Unless similar research instruments are used and the conditions of administration are replicated, it can be unwise to make more than very general comparisons between two survey samples.

After determining the character and scope of the insight you hope to gain, depending on local resources and expertise you may want to consider whether your goals can be fully or partially achieved using externally developed research initiatives. A number of these exist, including Project SAILS, LibQUAL+®, ClimateQUAL™, DigiQUAL®, MINES for Libraries™, COUNTER, and E-Metrics. Each is a fee-based proprietary research instrument administered by academic library systems to gain insight into local users and operations. All are developed by or allied with the Association of Research Libraries (ARL) Statistics & Measurement initiative (www.arl.org/stats/). As a producer of numerous library metrics and tracking programs, ARL also offers the "Effective, Sustainable, and

Practical Library Assessment" education service to encourage productive use of these measures in academic libraries. Externally produced measures tend to be rigorously tested, valid, and reliable, and typically include professionally produced reports that reduce the investment of staff time and resources.

LibQUAL+® and SAILS are two of the most widely used external assessment measures. Whereas many of the projects mentioned above focus on operational statistics (e.g., circulation statistics), LibQUAL+® and SAILS are user-focused research tools. Developed by ARL and the Texas A&M Libraries, the LibQUAL+® survey consists of roughly 20 questions and tests user perceptions of library service quality (www.libqual.org). Because it produces complicated metrics that involve a learning curve to fully interpret, participation in LibQUAL+® also entails training in results interpretation and other library evaluation strategies. LibQUAL+® is usually perceived as a longitudinal assessment measure, useful in benchmarking user satisfaction over time. Project SAILS is a web-based student information literacy assessment developed at Kent State University in Ohio (www.projectsails.org). Administered in partnership with ARL, the SAILS survey consists of 45 multiple-choice questions based on ACRL's *Information Literacy Competency Standards for Higher Education*. SAILS also functions as a longitudinal measure, and is useful for tracking the information competency of students as they progress through degree programs. Although the SAILS and LibQUAL+® survey instruments are standardized, each is somewhat customizable to reflect local characteristics and details.

While external measures investigate critical aspects of library education and service quality, they should not diminish the potential of customized local assessments. Developing a local environmental scan as part of a broader research strategy provides insight tailored to the goals and resources of a specific library. External instruments are highly valid and reliable, but they also may not provide the topical focus that will cover an institution's full range of research needs. Although Ohio University participates in both SAILS and LibQUAL+®, we found it necessary to undertake a local scan that dealt comprehensively with emerging technology tools and generated substantial open-ended feedback. Local inquiry complements externally provided research – findings of the OU scan provides a rich and insightful corollary to Ohio University LibQUAL+® and SAILS data.

Collaboration

Anyone who has been involved in institutional research knows that even the smallest venture can become a complex undertaking. User assessment in an institutional setting invariably requires the cooperation of multiple stakeholders, and the potential exists for layers of collaborative effort at every step in the process. Over the course of this project, I collaborated with members of the Reference and Instruction Technology Team and other library staff in a number of ways, inviting feedback and suggestions particularly while constructing survey instruments and conducting data analysis. While we welcomed the feedback of colleagues, I remained mindful that the surveys were developed largely within our department. This was intended not to exclude other stakeholders but to streamline the development process and allow us to keep a public service focus.

Had it more closely involved other campus or library partners, this project could doubtlessly have benefited in a number of ways. Expanding user research across organizational or departmental lines can add legitimacy, resources, and expertise. Research partnerships may provide outreach opportunities that form important allegiances across academic units and interest groups. Collaboration should be pursued with the understanding that project timelines can be extended as a result of added communication and coordination among stakeholders. Close partnerships with campus patterns can also reduce the library's topical "footprint" in survey content, and potentially open the project to more intensive human subjects review. The level of collaborative activity on a project should be determined at the outset rather than allowing other parties to effectively "jump on board" as the research develops. If close collaboration on library-initiated research is determined to be prohibitive, there are many opportunities to invite less intensive forms of feedback. Findings can also be shared among institutional partners with great success - despite the library-centric nature of our study, results have proven useful to several non-library constituents such as central campus Information Technology. By maintaining transparent independence throughout, we were able to keep a local focus while educating other stakeholders about library and technology interaction.

Choosing a Methodology

A survey is one of many ways to evaluate user expectations and prioritize emerging technologies. Some types of assessment are better suited for gauging the performance of a specific service or describing user experiences, while others more clearly portray broad participant beliefs, habits, and perceptions. Research methodologies are typically classified as either *quantitative*, *qualitative*, or *mixed-methods*. Quantitative research represents data through numerically descriptive means, qualitative research provides rich descriptions of contexts, users, and situations, and mixed-methods research generates both types of data. Some argue that because qualitative data can be "coded" and assigned to quantitative categories, that the distinction between these types of research is arbitrary, but from the perspective of selecting a research methodology there is a clear distinction between ethnographic and survey-based models. Both quantitative and qualitative methods can reveal unique characteristics of a user population, yet it is important to evaluate overall research goals and available resources against the strengths of your chosen method of data collection.

The Ohio University project employed web-based questionnaire methodology, one of the most common and accessible means of conducting an environmental scan. This type of survey research has the potential to generate a large participant sample, which provides the broadly generalizable feedback required for this type of assessment. A survey can be conducted online, in person, by mail, or by phone, but online and in-person administrations are the most feasible in an academic library setting. Depending on project aims and research questions, survey methodology can be supplemented or replaced by other types of assessment such as focus groups, usability testing, case studies, analytics, interviews, and participant observation. Table 3.1 presents a number of quantitative and qualitative research methods useful in practical research, outlining the type of data they produce and their most commonly perceived strengths and weaknesses.

Table 3.1 Comparing Research Methodologies

	Description	Strengths	Limitations	Data Type
Focus Groups	· guided discussion among 6-10 participants to gauge attitudes and beliefs	· provokes in-depth conversation · more efficient than individual interviews	· discussion can be derailed · outside facilitator may be necessary for objectivity and quality	· qualitative
Participant Observation	· close study and/ or recording of subjects engaged in tasks or using services in natural environments	· low intrusion on participants · realistic picture of user behavior · produces rich immersive descriptions	· observer can impact participant behavior · not all tasks can be easily observed · time-intensive · difficult to collate observer data	· qualitative
Interviews	· structured communication typically with one subject	· produces personal, detailed feedback · can allow for flexibility and greater depth of information	· time-intensive · low participation levels · hard to interpret and analyze · interviewer can influence response	· qualitative
Case Studies	· long-term observation of a single population or "case"	· provides in-depth information · change over time · offers multiple perspectives	· potentially expensive · long-term commitment · limited generalizability of results · narrowly focused	· qualitative
Questionnaires	· online, onsite, or telephone surveys using consistent questions	· large sample size · easy to analyze · produces consistent results	· impersonal · difficult to achieve desired response rates · may require incentives	· qualitative/ quantitative
Formal Action Research	· problem-based reflective process of data gathering and analysis	· dynamic and results-driven · productively focused · involves multiple research techniques	· complex process · involves multiple stakeholders and teamwork	· qualitative/ quantitative
Web Analytics	· analysis of website usage statistics provided by software such as Google Analytics	· offers real-world picture of user behavior · highlights high- and low-traffic areas of current web services	· portrays past and current use; difficult to predict future trends · tracks only behavior, user rationales not explored	· quantitative
Usability Testing	· gathering input on a service or product through realistic use scenarios	· produces detailed feedback · gauges real-world use and interaction	· observer influence data · time-consuming · requires controlled environment	· qualitative/ quantitative

Any of these methods can be developed independently or in tandem to create local studies that contribute to an overall environmental scan. When choosing a research methodology, the nature of the information you seek should be carefully weighed in order to select the most appropriate method(s). Are you interested in rich descriptions of user experiences and environments, or a broader understanding of use and access trends? Because each research design offers different types of insight, the most rigorous environmental scanning efforts will involve a number of methodologies in order to cast the most comprehensive net possible. For example, plans are underway to supplement the OU scan with a series of student focus groups at the department level. Focus groups can enhance survey findings with more personal, qualitative insight into how technology supports library services and operations.

Every research methodology has inherent strengths and limitations. Focus groups and interviews provide nuanced insight into user perceptions of libraries, but they also represent a smaller range of respondents, may not capture as full a picture of user opinion, and are subject to group dynamics. Ethnographic research such as participant observation may be the best way to immersively investigate a campus culture, but it is a complex and potentially long-term process that may not offer immediate insight to inform programmatic ventures. Long-term ethnographic research may also prove prohibitively expensive, and may even require full-time professional coordination. Questionnaire-based methods may most easily reach the largest number of users, but survey instruments must be carefully constructed to avoid bias and discourage inaccurate self-representation. Data analysis presents challenges for the novice, and results intended for broad distribution will need to be presented in concise and understandable formats.

Case Study: Ohio University

The remainder of this chapter focuses on the development and administration of the web-based survey project conducted by the Ohio University Libraries in 2008. While a close examination of the research methods outlined in Table 3.1 falls outside the scope of this report, there are a number of resources that provide more in-depth treatment for those interested in pursuing other methods. Radford and Snelson's recent *Academic Library Research: Perspectives and Current Trends* provides insight into broad changes and trends in many areas of library research. Powell and Conaway's *Basic Research Methods for Librarians* or Creswell's *Research Design: Qualitative, Quantitative, and Mixed Methods Approaches* provide library and non-library perspectives on the research process. For those considering qualitative or ethnographic research, Foster and Gibbons' *Studying Students: the Undergraduate Research Project at the University of Rochester* provides an excellent example of library ethnography. For in-depth discussions of qualitative methodology, consult Creswell's *Qualitative Inquiry and Research Design: Choosing Among Five Approaches*.

Research Design

After selecting web-based survey methodology as the best way to pursue our scope and purpose, I began to develop a research design. A research design is the specific strategy constructed to gather and analyze user feedback, and in a practical research is a relatively informal process. A research design is a more detailed treatment of the chosen methodology, and should produce the series of steps that will guide the research itself. Systematic planning is essential to creating sound and scalable assessments in general. A fundamental aspect of the planning process is establishing a clear project timeline, which has the effect of aligning the research with predetermined goals. It is good practice to keep a log or record of your project scope, purpose, research design, goals, timeline, and so forth in order to more easily communicate this information during the reporting phase of the project – for example, a shared Google Document works well for this purpose.

Variables and Research Questions

Defining research questions is an important part of the design process. Research questions can be detailed, hard and fast, or somewhere in between, but they should always provide a template for the topics that will be covered by the actual survey instruments. The corollary to creating research questions is the identification of concretely investigable variables. In practical research, identifying research questions and specifying variables is a complementary process that provides the structure for a questionnaire.

Scalability comes into play when designing research questions and specifying variables, another aspect of environmental scanning that can be relatively informal. Because my analysis of the data would be both practical and rigorous, I created the following series of formal research questions to illuminate how and why students perceived and interacted with libraries and technology:

1) What are the technology profiles (defined as technology ownership, use, skill, and adoption status) of Ohio University students?

2) What are the library profiles (defined as library use, skill, awareness, and emerging technology receptivity) of Ohio University students?

3) How do the library and technology profiles of students of disparate demographic factors such as age, digital status, major, gender, and academic status differ?

4) How can student receptiveness to and awareness of emerging technology library services be characterized?

5) How do students of disparate library and technology profiles compare in their awareness of, assessment of, and receptivity to traditional and emerging technology-based library services?

6) Does overall facility with technology affect the student library experience?

7) What is the relationship between student use and awareness of library services and self-perception of technological competency, research skill, and receptivity to emerging technologies?

Defining these research questions proved invaluable to the construction of survey instrument items, helped focus the process of data analysis, and provided the context to communicate survey findings. Each question was constructed in order to reveal relationships between dependent and independent variables. Variables are traits, characteristics and entities that can be measured and reflect a range of values, such age, number of hours spent online per week, social networking software preference, and so forth. Considering variables is helpful when trying to determine what questions to include and how to word answer options. All variables fall under two broad categories – quantitative (measuring naturally numerical values such as GPA, income, number of gaming devices owned) and categorical (measuring things that are not naturally quantified, such as academic status, number of gaming devices owned etc.). Variables lend themselves to different types of analysis according to the scales they use to measure value (e.g. least to most, 1 through 5, yes or no, multiple choice, etc). Because these values determine how data can be statistically analyzed, it is important to carefully consider the range of answers each variable will produce. For my formal analysis, dependent variables were the library-specific characteristics I expected would be affected by differences in the independent variables, or the technological and demographic characteristics of the respondents. For practical analysis, variables described demographic and other characteristics I used to conduct cross-tabulations.

Independent Variables:
Technology profile (**ownership**, **use**, **skill**, and **technology adoption status**)
Demographic profile (**age**, **digital status**, **academic status**, **major**, and **gender**)
Dependent Variables:
Library profile (**use**, **skill**, **perceptions**, and **emerging technology receptivity**)

Hypothesizing around variables and research questions is a central component of formal research, but is not required of practical research projects. The goal of practical studies should be to create an achievable research design that creates local knowledge and informs operations, meaning that establishing testable hypotheses is not absolutely necessary.

Instrument Construction and Distribution

Creating a valid questionnaire or survey instrument that produces reliable information is challenging, and in a practical research context the amount of time devoted to instrument design should be weighed in terms of scalability. There are a number of kinds of validity in research, all focused on creating consistent and reliable responses. If you are conducting a simple, small-scale user poll in order to gather opinions regarding a small service change, agonizing over question wording, type, and validity is somewhat less important. If your results will be widely read, distributed, published, and/or will affect library policy in meaningful ways, it is important to design your survey instrument carefully. It is always necessary to consider the ends to which your findings will be used – any librarian who regularly conducts surveys knows that results have a way of working their way through an organization. Appendix A provides a sample questionnaire comprised of items gathered from the original two instruments used in the OU environmental scanning project. This sample survey features annotations on a number of question types, and provides general insights into questionnaire design. The original content and answer choices from the Ohio surveys has been updated and revised to create a current template better suited for adaptation at other institutions.

Survey topics were determined by a collaborative method of brainstorming, drafting reviewing, honing, and revising. The Technology Team and Reference Department staff pooled ideas to identify the broadest range of current and emerging technologies and trends, library use scenarios, and potential library technology applications. I then considered how each of these could be best explored by question type and constructed a draft questionnaire, which I then submitted to the Technology Team, other staff, and a College of Education Faculty member for review and revision. The content definition process was open to library-wide feedback particularly during the second survey, which focused on student use of the library website and facilities. In order to gather this feedback I created a page on the Ohio University staff wiki that allowed interested staff to submit suggestions. At the conclusion of the project, I made survey reports and findings available in the same space.

As Appendix A illustrates, questionnaires were comprised of a range of question types, such as rating scales, multiple choice, short answer, and so forth. A comprehensive examination of questionnaire construction, answer scales, and item types is beyond the scope of this paper, but I can communicate several suggestions that may be useful when designing a survey instrument. The language used to word questions is an important aspect of survey design, particularly when one is dealing with a sample population that spans numerous age or other demographic groups. When crafting each item, be conscious of the formality or informality of your language and how it might affect the way your respondents answer. Being overly formal may alienate or confuse some younger respondents, whereas excessive familiarity or informality may have the opposite effect for audiences who expect a certain type of language from surveys. As a rule, attempt to tailor your language so that it will be accessible to the full range of possible respondents while remaining unbiased, measured, and neutral. In order to try to sustain attention and elicit accurate responses, I created questionnaires that used relatively informal language while still maintaining objectivity and clarity. Regardless of your intended audience or the type of question selected, the objective meaning of each should emerge rather than the language or interests of the designer. Avoiding ambiguity is key, as is designing answer choices that lend themselves to clear analysis. For more detailed treatment of questionnaire design and related matters, consult Rea and Parker's *Designing and Conducting Survey Research: A Comprehensive Guide*.

Questionnaires and student responses were managed with the Libraries' local online survey management application, phpESP 1.8.2. Administered from January 9, 2008, to February 15, 2008, Student Technology Survey 1 consisted of 55 primarily closed-form multiple-choice items covering a broad range of technology and library-related topics. Student Technology Survey 2 was administered from May 15 to June 15, 2008, and consisted of 22 open response and multiple-choice items that covered library service, information, and facility use. A total of 3,648 respondents or roughly 18% of the student population completed the first online questionnaire, while 1,651 or roughly 8% completed the second. This disparity can be explained in part by the makeup of the surveys themselves. The first questionnaire consisted largely of closed-form questions, while the second invited more open-ended commentary. Open-ended questions usually involve more respondent time and mental investment, and are sometimes seen as a detriment to survey completion a (see Appendix A). Several items were included in both instruments as a content validity measure and to enable accurate demographic reporting of sample populations. In order to ensure their accuracy within both user needs assessment and formal research contexts, questionnaires were reviewed by Reference and Instruction Department librarians, submitted for analysis by a College of Education faculty member, and administered on "trial run" basis with student employees prior to their release. Stylistic, content, and grammatical changes were made based on feedback from each group.

Online applications such as SurveyMonkey, Zoomerang, QuestionPro, PollDaddy, and Google Forms (part of Google Documents) can streamline the process of designing survey research. Some applications are more powerful than others, and it is frequently the case that advanced question and analysis features require a subscription or purchase. For example, a basic 10-question survey can be created using the free version of SurveyMonkey, but more in-depth analysis and reporting features are only available with an individual or institutional membership. Each application should be examined for its strengths and weaknesses, which can have a significant impact on how a survey is designed. For example, the technical limitations of phpESP prevented us from creating multi-answer question matrices like those used throughout Appendix A. In the case of the first survey this highly preferable question type could have reduced the overall number of questionnaire items and created a more concise instrument, one of the most important methods for increasing sample returns.

Promotion and Distribution

The distribution and promotion of a survey has a great deal of impact on the size and character of the respondent sample it generates, and consequently on the overall generalizability of findings. Large technology surveys such as those conducted by ECAR and OCLC are typically administered to randomly generated groups of respondents within specific population parameters. If survey participants are randomly selected, responses are thought to be more representative of the overall population. If a survey sample is not randomly generated, its conclusions are considered to be nonscientific and less generalizable to other populations due to inherent bias within a self-selected sample. What is known as an *elective convenience sample* is typically the most feasible way to generate participation in a local library setting, and was the non-random method used by the OU project. Campus-wide emails, postings in the Library News blog, word of mouth, instruction session mentions, and long-term links on the Ohio University Libraries home page promoted each survey. Students were offered financial incentives to participate in each survey - three randomly selected students received $100 at the conclusion of Survey 1, and one received $100 at the conclusion of Survey 2. Survey 1 experienced twice the return rate of Survey 2, overall response to each survey far exceeded expectations. Financial or other incentives are often perceived to be the best motivators for survey participation. If random participant selection is not considered critical to a local scanning project, eye-catching articles or posts that prominently feature information on a survey incentive are excellent ways to increase rates of return. With permission, I used images of the first survey's winners to promote the second survey (Figure 3.1).

Based on responses to an item included in each questionnaire, ninety-three percent of respondents learned about the survey by email, 5% from the library website, and 2% via word of mouth. As this unequal discovery distribution indicates, campus-wide student, staff, and faculty email lists are promising are avenues for survey promotion. If campus communication via email list is restricted, other methods may be available such as student news sources, LMS messages, and advertising in social network sites. Each of these promotional avenues should be considered for how they may shape the overall survey sample.

Figure 3.1: Promotional Blog Post Featuring Incentive Winners

Ohio University Libraries News
News and Events from Alden Library

« Friends of the Libraries Book Sale May 8-10, 2008
Library Awards: Research and Creative Activity Expo, 2008 »

Students, this could be you! Another chance at $100.

Check out ``and`` - two of our **$100 winners** from last quarter's **Library Technology Survey**.

If you didn't take the first survey, or if you didn't win last time - please stop crying! You have another chance to **win $100** from the OU Libraries, just by taking the second installment of our anonymous survey. This one is **much** shorter, and should only take **5 minutes** or so of your time:

click here to take the survey!

The survey will be open until **June 14th**, and we'll draw the winner on **June 15th**. (We'll mail the check to the winner if they're not in town over the summer.)

Categories
» Events (42)
» Exhibits (14)
» Friends of the Libraries (32)
» General (98)
» People (5)
» Podcasts (4)
» Resources (55)
» Services (29)
» New Library Acquisitions

Search:
[Search]

Archives
» June 2008
» May 2008
» April 2008
» March 2008
» February 2008

Analysis

There are many ways of conducting statistical analysis, most of which are unnecessary for interpreting the results of practical evaluation. Local research does not necessarily require anything more than the ability to produce and interpret basic graphs and tables in order to effectively communicate the results of a survey. Basic statistical methods of description and crosstabulation are the foundation of the majority of library-based research, and neither calls for statistical expertise. Descriptives list the simple distribution of responses to an item (e.g., average number of Facebook applications used), while cross-tabulation segments these responses based on one of more demographic characteristics (e.g., number of Facebook applications used by age, gender, and academic major) Typically, online survey software such as SurveyMonkey will automatically produce a summary of descriptive data at the close of a poll or survey. Many also have built-in features to assist in cross-tabulating data, a powerful method for separating and comparing the responses of specific user communities. Finally, these programs allow you to export data in order to analyze it in more powerful programs such as SPSS, a standard statistical application used in the social sciences.

After the collection phase of each survey, I began the process of analyzing response data. I exported total responses from our survey software package into what is known as a comma separated value (CSV) file, both as an important backup measure and in order to prepare raw responses. If anything beyond the summary analysis conducted within a survey software package will occur, data sets must be coded, reviewed, and "cleaned up" in order to spot errors and assign variables that lend themselves to investigation by a specific program.

In order to produce the findings described in Chapters 4-7, I conducted statistical analyses on each response set using SPSS 14.0 and 16.0 using a number of analytical methods. Basic *frequencies* and *descriptives* summarize total responses for each item, while *crosstabulation* segments data into demographic subsets by age, academic status, digital status, gender, and technology adoption status (early, mainstream, and late). In order to produce *correlation* analyses of concepts such as library and technology use, ownership, skill, perceptions, and awareness in Tables 4.1-4.2 and 7.2-7.3, I recoded and combined the data into a series of scales and indexes, described in detail in Appendix B. Figure 3.2 provides an example of working with variable cross-tabulation in SPSS. Two excellent primers on using SPSS for data analysis are Morgan, Leech, Gleckner, and Barrett's *SPSS for Introductory Statistics: Use and Interpretation*, and Daniel Muijs' *Doing Quantitative Research in Education: with SPSS*.

Because SPSS requires data to have numerical values in order to be analyzed, it was necessary to use Microsoft Excel to "code" verbatim responses to open-ended survey items. For the three questions in Survey 2 that asked participants to describe the best and worst aspects of the OU Libraries and offer general comments, myself and two other departmental staff individually hand-coded approximately 5,000 short-answer responses, assigning numerical values to a range of categories that described the content of their answers and "triangulating" our results to ensure accuracy. These categories assigned were produced through a collaborative process of reviewing a subset of responses and arriving at consensus on the main topics that emerged. For a more detailed treatment of statistical methods in library research, Hafner's *Descriptive Statistical Techniques for Librarians* is a useful resource.

Figure 3.2: SPSS Crosstabulation Analysis

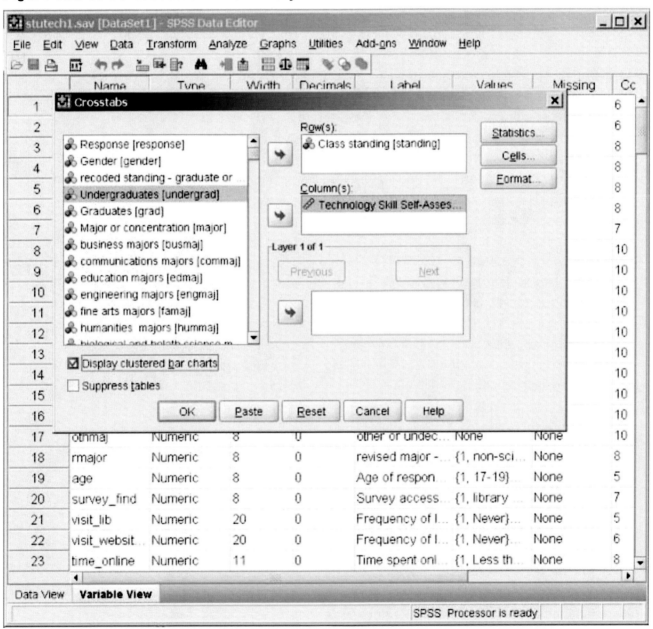

Communicating Results

It is essential to communicate survey findings clearly and comprehensibly and the production of a survey report is often a critical aspect of an environmental scan. I produced several documents in conjunction with the OU study, including an executive summary and detailed report of findings that were made available throughout the Ohio University Libraries and to other interested parties at Ohio University. I also presented survey findings in an open library forum. The formal Master's of Education report I created in conjunction with the OU scan provided the foundation of this published document, which has been adapted and expanded to incorporate a focus on best practices and implications for other libraries. My former colleague Chris Guder and I also presented a 2009 ACRL Conference paper that reported an overview of survey findings and considered practical outcomes of the Student Technology Survey at Ohio University Libraries (Booth & Guder, 2009).

Creating comprehensible, readable tables and graphics can be assisted by consulting examples as well as by studying principles of visual communication. I recommend reading national survey reports such as those produced by OCLC, the Pew Internet & American Life project, and ECAR for inspiration on graph and table design. The works of Edward Tufte (*The Visual Display of Quantitative Information, Envisioning Information, Beautiful Evidence, Visual Explanations: Images and Quantities, Evidence and Narrative*) provide an important foundation in the presentation of quantitative data, while Lidwell, Holden, and Butler's *Universal Principles of Design* describes a number of core concepts in effective visual design.

A drawback of survey-based inquiry is that it is often difficult or uninteresting for those uninvolved in the research itself to interpret the full extent and implication of its findings – it is therefore important to ensure that there are multiple opportunities for peer- and self-education in a situation of this kind. Data sets can be used in a number of ways, and a formal report is not the only deliverable of local research. In order to maximize the impact of our findings, a complete spreadsheet of coded verbatim responses to evaluation questions was widely distributed to library departments, which allowed them to see the specific respondent suggestions, praise, and criticism that pertained to their units.

Another unexpectedly powerful application of this project occurred on the level of one-on-one data consultations with subject and outreach librarians. As one of the analysis procedures associated with this project, I invited library staff with outreach interest in a specific segment of the survey population (first-year students, graduate students, Literature and Theater majors, etc) to sit down with me after reviewing the final report and, using SPSS, create customized on-the-fly user profiles. Via cross-tabulation analysis, I compared demographic variables such as age, academic major, and academic status to any other factors the subject specialist found interesting, such as student use of various Google tools, frequency of library website visits, self-assessment of research skills, and so forth. When benchmarked against the respondent sample as a whole (a default feature of SPSS cross-tabulations), these customized profiles provided rare insight into specific users and identified areas of outreach potential within different student populations.

Appendix B is an example of the SPSS output file created during an on-the-fly consultation I held with OU First-Year Outreach Librarian Sherri Saines. This customized "student library/technology profile" illustrates the responses of first-year students compared to total respondents based on a number of questions that Saines brainstormed during her initial read-through of the overall findings report, a document that allowed her to generate a sense of what variables were studied and why. As she relayed inquiries about her population of interest (e.g., *How frequently do first-years use library computers relative to other users? Are first-years more or less confident in their research skills?*), I performed crosstabulation analyses of relevant variables to rapidly create the series of tables in Appendix B. Saines and I discussed these as they were created, interpreting statistics and considering implications and questions raised by each graphic.

These responsive, tailored statistical treatments proved to be one of the most valuable forms of analysis I conducted. A series of one-on-one consultations expanded the range of insight staff gained from the data, and allowed interested parties to interact with pertinent aspects of the findings in a way that would not have been possible from even an extensive report. Instead of confronting a static series of inscrutable percentages, Saines, others, and I were able to fluidly create interpretable statistical portraits of specific user communities, producing documents similar to Appendix B as lasting evidence of our conversations. I highly encourage others to interact as creatively and with as much depth as possible with data sets, and to consider findings as sources of ongoing and multifaceted insight.

Research Limitations

There are many types of inherent and inevitable error associated with the research process, and it is important to be aware of the limitations of your method(s) in order to gain a realistic perspective on information provided. Doing so can prevent you from reaching false conclusions or assuming that results are flawless and/or more representative than they actually are. No study can be so thorough as to provide anything but an incomplete window of insight into your users. Results must be taken with a grain of salt, and should be analyzed as closely for what they fail to capture or communicate as for what they succeed in discovering. Combining different types of methodologies will result in the most complete base of understanding – using multiple groups, conducting interviews to supplement questionnaires, or conducting an annual study to track results over time are all ways to gain fuller understanding into user perceptions, traits, and behaviors.

Whether a study is intended for peer-reviewed publication or for informal local use, it is good practice to identify and address limitations when writing up your findings, which allows your audience to consider and interpret potential caveats. An ethic of critical self-disclosure is a best practice aspect of any research – as much can be learned from what goes awry during the assessment process as by what goes smoothly. Cultivating the ability to stand up to your own close questioning will help you explain and defend the results of your efforts to others. On a broader scale, library cultures of assessment should value this and other types of "failure" as readily as they celebrate success, recognizing the inherent function of mistakes to provide learning opportunities.

The following factors can be considered potential caveats to the reliability and validity of our research project. The Ohio University Libraries are distinct from many Association of Research

Libraries (ARL) member institutions in a number of ways. Physical facilities are unusually centralized - Alden Library, a 7-floor, 2-million volume main building, houses the majority of collections and subject libraries. Combined with a small Music and Dance Library and an offsite storage facility, Alden serves a campus of almost 21,000 students. Despite a new university student center, the historic lack of campus study and social space paired with the relatively recent construction of a popular 24-hour Learning Commons has resulted in heavy use of library facilities. This may have introduced respondents to a range of services that are typically more dispersed throughout a number of library branches, potentially creating a high level of service awareness or receptiveness. If true, this could further limit the applicability of these results to more distributed or less frequented library systems.

Findings are based on questionnaires distributed primarily by an all-student email message, generating a non-random sample that likely represents a section of the Ohio University student body modestly skewed towards greater technology competency. Because its respondent base was self-selected, the statistical validity and reliability of survey results cannot be considered explicitly "scientific". That said, instruments were created to a reasonable degree of precision, and the considerable sample size of this study both increases its generalizability to the Ohio University population as a whole and decreases its overall margin of error.

Due to the exclusively online format and distribution of the survey, the respondents may have possessed greater levels of familiarity with web-based communication methods. To mitigate *sampling bias* towards the heavily technology-oriented and/or frequent campus email users, each survey was made available for four weeks and concurrently promoted on the library website, news blog, and in library instruction sessions. Some degree of *self-selection bias* in the sample population may also reasonably be assumed. Those motivated to participate may have done so because of their existing relationship to the Libraries and resulting positive or negative impressions thereof. Although the vast majority of responses originated in library-neutral space (email, as opposed to the library news blog), the Libraries were identified in the subject line as survey sponsors. The study was functionally anonymous, but it is likely that *social desirability bias* motivated some participants to intentionally or unintentionally respond in ways that misrepresented their actual interaction with or opinion of the subjects.

Demographic data for younger students is tracked in smaller age increments than it is for older students, so those under 27 were segmented into 4 categories and respondents over 31 are presented as one cohort. This grouping facilitates more granular analysis of the youngest respondents and allowed the segmentation of all participants into categories of digital natives and immigrants in order to test the soundness of generational assumptions. It also necessitated that older students are portrayed in a less detailed fashion. Participation in both surveys was not mandatory to qualify for offered incentives, and although some degree of overlap is likely, it can be assumed that a majority of unique participants exist between Surveys 1 and 2. Respondents in the second survey were slightly older on average and reported marginally higher library use rates relative to those in the first, likely due to the mid-quarter release of the second survey relative to the early-quarter release of the first. Survey software provided no means of tracking unsuccessful or abandoned attempts at completion, making it difficult to determine whether user or system error or lack of familiarity with web-based instruments deterred a significant number of participants.

Due to its foundations in survey methodology, the conclusions drawn by this project are based almost entirely on student self-perceptions, self-disclosure, and self-assessments rather than on objective evaluation or demonstrated use of the technologies and topics in question. As such, its findings should be considered with the same degree of scrutiny as similar studies. A recent article in the *Chronicle of Higher Education* warns that research based on student skill self-assessments should be considered potentially capricious; aspects of the present study fall under this heading (Schmidt, 2008). This should not cause the reader to question the degree to which this report provides insight into the library and technology cultures of respondents, however. Findings faithfully reflect the diversity of opinions expressed by students in regards to these cultures and the way they shape their experiences of higher education.

Findings and Implementation

The Technology Team pursued this research out of a desire to base service decisions on demonstrated levels of current and anticipated student library and technology use. Findings have provided considerable and often unexpected knowledge into the library and technology cultures of OU students, which had the immediate effect of demystifying many of the typically confusing questions raised by the largest academic library user group. *How often do students visit the physical library? What technologies do they own, and how do they use these tools for research? Are they open to library services in Facebook, or would they rather their academic pursuits be completely separate from their social online environments?* Beyond this baseline insight, findings have provided a practical foundation for approaching services throughout the library from the vantage point of informed and strategic cost-benefit analysis. The practical implementations of survey findings will likely continue to reveal themselves indefinitely as the Libraries evaluate their performance against user expectations.

The conclusion of this project coincided with my transition to a new position with the UC Berkeley Libraries, but through communication with my former coworkers I have tracked how this project has influenced library service and policy decisions. As a result of this project, the Technology Team has a clearer working timeline of potential student adoption of numerous emerging technologies, which has translated into action on a number of fronts. Facebook services, and LMS library integration, library widgets, and library browser toolbars are all now regarded as priority areas for student-focused development, and all have been pursued with initially positive results (Wilson, in press). MySpace library activity has been all but eschewed, our Skype pilots are under evaluation, and plans for an OPAC text messaging services are underway.

Based on the analysis of responses to open-ended items in Survey 2, a number of facility, policy, and procedural changes have been made or are currently under investigation. Student expectations for computing facilities, quiet areas, and extended hours were among the first to be addressed, and as a direct result of respondent feedback more workstations have been placed in designated quiet areas on the first and fifth floors of Alden Library. In addition, overnight public user access to the Learning Commons is now restricted, and based on student frustration regarding "camping" at library computers individual stations now log users out after a certain amount of inactivity. A second overnight floor in the main library is also under consideration in order to address student desires for additional computer stations, increased group and individual study space, and expanded quiet study areas. Smaller practical suggestions such as additional bulletin boards for student announcements and more prominent and browsable leisure reading sections are also being discussed. Finally and perhaps most importantly, the sense of collective appreciation and goodwill communicated via the deluge of positive open-ended comments had the widespread effect of validating our personal and organizational efforts, which can be counted among the survey project's most indispensable results.

Part II: A Case Study in Environmental Scanning

Chapter 4: Participant Demographics

As service organizations, academic libraries should understand and cater to the actual (as opposed to the imagined or predicted) needs of their users. This project investigated common assumptions regarding student use and receptivity to technology and libraries to inform emerging service prioritization in the context of Ohio University Readers should interpret these results as characteristic of environmental scanning, which produces a detailed view of the needs and traits of a specific population that can be used to increase understanding and inform future decisions. By presenting the Ohio University findings, I hope to add to the library technology debate by illustrating the power and specificity of insight that can be gained by examining various tools and services from a localized perspective. Contextual investigation reveals complexity behind the oft-cited blanket "user" generalization, and provides opportunities for actionable ends based on user feedback.

The summary of survey findings is presented in four chapters. Chapter 4 explains the demographic makeup of the survey sample, Chapter 5 presents the *Student Technology Cultures* that emerged from the scan, Chapter 6 describes *Student Library Cultures*, and Chapter 7 presents findings related to *Students and Library Technology Receptivity*. Throughout these chapters, I pursue three objectives:

1) Provide a localized snapshot of the information and technology climate of Ohio University and its effect on the student library experience.
2) Examine generational and other demographic assumptions that influenced our perceptions and responses to students and technology.
3) Reveal factors that affect local student receptiveness to emerging library technologies.

Study Setting

Ohio University and its library system are generally representative of medium to large doctoral research universities in the United States. Ohio University consists of seven branches with a main campus located in Athens, Ohio. The Athens campus enrolls approximately 21,000 students and employs 1,200 faculty members. Eighty-eight percent of students are undergraduates, 12% are graduate and medical students, and enrollment by gender is roughly equivalent (51% female to 49% male). The Ohio University Libraries employ roughly 100 FTE, hold a collection of close to 3 million volumes, and were among the founding members of the OhioLINK consortium. Although the library system is affiliated with several regional OU campuses, enrollment at the Athens campus was required for participation in the Student Technology Survey.

Demographic Breakdown

Unless otherwise indicated, combined responses from identical test items replicated in Surveys 1 and 2 comprise demographic and library use data. Percentages in narrative descriptions and tables may at times not equal 100% due to rounding or the availability of multiple response items. A total of 5,299 responses were received to the two surveys administered in this project (N1=3,648; N2=1,651). Seventy-six percent of respondents were 22 years old or younger, 12% were between 23 and 27, 5% were aged 27 through 30, and the remaining 6% represented the 31 and older student demographic (Figure 4.1).

As I described in Definition of Terms and Chapter 2, Presnky's generational dichotomy divides individuals born before and after 1980? in to two separate classes, *digital immigrants* and *digital natives*. Employing this as a demographic variable for testing assumptions regarding generational library and technology characteristics, 88% (N=4,728) of the sample population can be considered *digital natives* (born during or after 1981) while the remaining 12% (N=571) can be considered *digital immigrants* (born before 1981**).**

Figure 4.1 Participants by Age

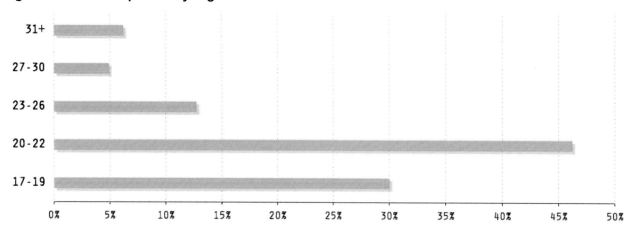

Approximately 81% percent of total survey participants were undergraduate students, 16% were graduate or medical students, and 3% were "non-traditional" or non-degree seeking students (Figure 4.2). Considerably more respondents were female than male, 61% v. 39%, (Figure 4.3). Despite this gender disparity, respondents are a relatively representative cross-section of academic disciplines at Ohio University, with heaviest participation from students in Communications, the Social Sciences, Business, Education, and the combined Life/Health Sciences (Figure 4.4).

Figure 4.2 Participants by Status

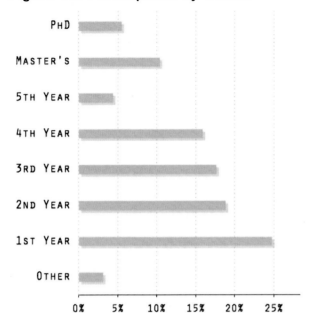

Figure 4.3 Participants by Gender

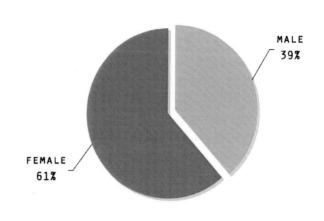

Figure 4.4 Participants by Discipline

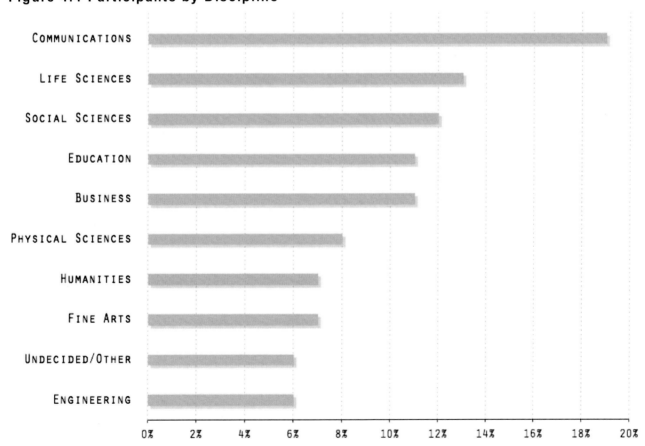

Academic Status v. Digital Status

Tables 4.1-4.2 use correlation analysis to establish the strength of the relationship between *digital status* and *academic status* among participants in Survey 1, demographic categories that are often conflated in discussions of library users and technology development.

A Note on Interpreting Correlations

Correlation analysis is a statistical technique useful in illuminating relationships between of variables. While much can be learned from correlations, a common maxim cautions against using them deductively: "correlation does not imply causation." A correlation between two variables describes the nature and strength of their relationship, but it cannot indicate whether one variable "caused" another. Predicting and explaining relationships is the function of regression and other types of analysis. Whereas correlation is a *descriptive* statistical technique, regression analysis is *inferential*. Descriptive statistics simply describe data, while inferential statistics may be used to test hypotheses and make causal connections based on data. The goal of my research was to describe observed behaviors and relationships, and therefore inferential analysis falls outside the scope of this project.

Correlation analysis measures two things: 1) the *extent* to which two variables are associated, and 2) the *direction* of that association. *Direction* is indicated by whether a correlation is positive or negative. A positively valued correlation indicates that as one variable increases the other variable increases (e.g. the lower the birth year of respondents, the greater the likelihood that they are graduate students). A negatively valued correlation indicates an inverse relationship, meaning that as one variable increases the other decreases (e.g. the higher the birth year of respondents, the lower the likelihood that they are graduate students). A correlation is positive so long as the direction of the effect it describes is the same, whereas a correlation is negative so long as the direction of the effect it describes is opposite.

The association between two variables is indicated by a value ranging between 1.0 and -1.0. A perfect positive correlation between two variables would be 1.0, whereas a perfect negative correlation would be -1.0. One additional thing correlations can suggest is whether a particular connection between two variables is likely or not likely to have occurred by chance. A relationship that is so weak that it could easily happen by accident is "statistically insignificant." A relationship that is strong enough to be very unlikely to be random is "statistically significant." The extent or "strength" of a connection between two variables is indicated by the size of the decimal that associates them. An association of .000 indicates no relationship, and a value of .100 is quite weak. In contrast a value of .900 is very strong, while 1.00 is strongest. A discussion of multiple correlation analysis will follow in Chapter 7.

In this study, the *digital status* variable divides participants into native/immigrants categories by age, while the *academic status* variable divides them into undergraduate and graduate categories by academic standing. Because both academic and digital status are ordinally scaled variables (ranked by non-numerical degree) and not normally distributed (do not fall on a typical bell-shaped distribution curve), I selected Kendall's Tau-b as the most appropriate statistic to investigate connections between them (Morgan, 2004).

Table 4.1 Correlation of Academic Status with Digital Status (N1)

			Academic Status	Digital Status
Kendall's tau_b	Academic Status	Correlation Coefficient	1.000	.583**
		Sig. (2-tailed)	.	.000
		N	3558	3558
	Digital Status	Correlation Coefficient	.583**	1.000
		Sig. (2-tailed)	.000	.
		N	3558	3648

**. Correlation is significant at the 0.01 level (2-tailed).

Table 4.2 Cross-Tabulation of Academic Status with Digital Status (N1)

		Digital Status		
		Native	Immigrant	Total
Undergraduate	Count	2906	60	2966
	Expected Count	2676	289	2966
	% within Academic Status	98%	2%	100%
	% within Digital Status	91%	17%	83%
Graduate	Count	305	287	592
	Expected Count	534	57	592
	% within Academic Status	51%	48%	100%
	% within Digital Status	10%	83%	16%
Total	Count	3211	347	3558
	Expected Count	3211	347	3558
	% within Academic Status	90%	10%	100%

The above analysis suggests a moderately strong significant relationship between the two variables (tau= .583, p=<.001), indicating a clear but by no means exclusive connection between digital native and undergraduate academic status. Table 4.2 illustrates the extent of the digital status disparity that exists between graduate and undergraduate populations. Only 2% of undergraduate students in this survey can be characterized as digital immigrants according to Prensky's definition, whereas approximately 51% of graduate students can be characterized as digital natives. For this reason, academic and digital status can be compared but not equated.

Chapter 5: Student Technology Cultures

A goal of the Student Technology Survey was to create an accurate and insightful portrayal of the various technology cultures apparent among Ohio University students, which I define as consisting of student attitudes, perceptions, needs, and expectations in respect to a range of information, computing, and communication tools. Described here as the overall Student Technology Profile, findings are presented in four sections: 5.1 Ownership, 5.2 Use, 5.3 Skill, and 5.4 Adoption.

5.1: Technology Ownership

Hardware

Students in Survey 1 were asked to indicate ownership of a range of common computing and communication devices and methods. Twenty-seven percent of students reported owning a desktop computer, whereas 84% owned a laptop (Figure 5.1). Twenty-three percent of respondents were Mac users, while 77% used Windows-based platforms. Roughly 1% used Unix or Linux machines, equivalent to the number unsure what type of operating system they used. Ninety-four percent owned a cell phone, while 80% owned an iPod or MP3 player. Only 6% reported owning a "smartphone" such as a Blackberry or iPhone, while 4% owned a PDA or similar device. Of cell phone users, 80% sent text messages. Over 40%of students owned a gaming console such as a XBOX or PlayStation, and close to 10% owned a portable gaming device such as a Nintendo DS.

Figure 5.1 Student Technology Ownership by Device

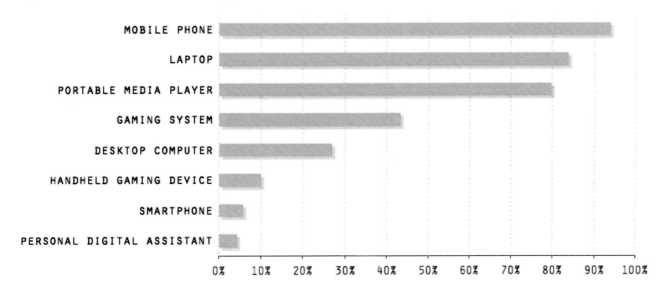

Ohio University students reflect a trend among higher education students towards increasing ownership of mobile technologies such as laptops, cell phones, and handheld gaming devices, illustrated over time by the 2004-2008 ECAR Study of Undergraduate Students and Information Technology. Figure 5.2 demonstrates that when segmented by digital status, younger students were on average more likely to own more information and communication technology devices than older students, but that digital immigrants were slightly more likely to own the greatest number of total devices listed in figure 5.1 (6-8 total). On average, respondents 26 and younger owned 3-5 technology devices, whereas those 27 and older owned 2-4.

Figure 5.2 Number of Devices Owned by Digital Status

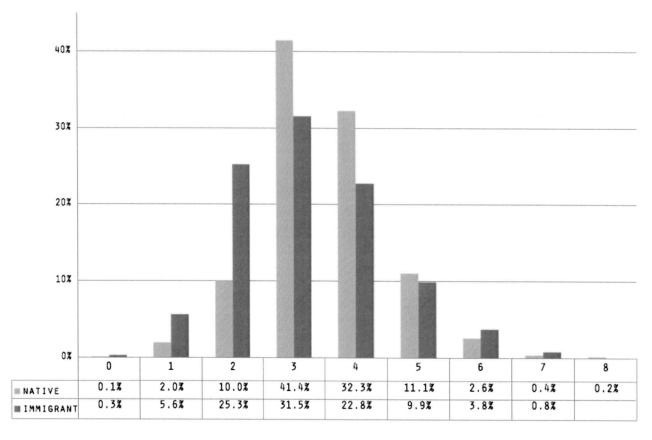

	0	1	2	3	4	5	6	7	8
NATIVE	0.1%	2.0%	10.0%	41.4%	32.3%	11.1%	2.6%	0.4%	0.2%
IMMIGRANT	0.3%	5.6%	25.3%	31.5%	22.8%	9.9%	3.8%	0.8%	

Disparate technology ownership by digital native and immigrant respondents tends to confirm research into generational differences and information and communication technology use. Younger respondents were much more likely to own gaming systems and mobility-based technologies such as cell phones and portable media players, although laptop ownership was consistently high between groups (Table 5.1). Respondents 27 and older were twice as likely to own a desktop computer or a PDA than those 26 and younger, and half as likely to own a gaming system. Ninety-five percent of digital natives owned mobile phones, compared to 86% of digital immigrants.

Table 5.1 Device Ownership by Digital Status

	Native	Immigrant
Desktop computer	24%	55%
Laptop	84%	81%
Portable media player	83%	55%
Mobile phone	95%	86%
Smartphone	6%	5%
Personal digital assistant	4%	9%
Gaming system	45%	23%
Handheld gaming device	10%	8%

Console and Handheld Gaming

Survey 2 asked participants to indicate ownership of a range of handheld and console video gaming devices. Figure 5.3 represents the percentage of the student population that reported ownership of each type of console or handheld, indicating that the overall prevalence of gaming among students is quite high. Although 44% of total respondents did not own any type of system, 23% owned one piece of gaming equipment, 16% owned two, and 17% of total respondents owned three or more gaming consoles or handhelds. A breakdown of video gaming device ownership shows that students were most likely to own a Sony PlayStation 2 and least likely to own a PlayStation 3 (PS3). Surprisingly, fully 31% of respondents reported owning an "oldschool Sega, Nintendo, or Atari system," more than those who owned a PlayStation 2 or 3 at the time of the survey. It is unclear whether students were in physical possession of these legacy gaming systems, or if they were located at a childhood home. In addition to consoles and handheld gaming, 34% percent of respondents indicated that they played games online.

Figure 5.3 Ownership of Gaming Devices

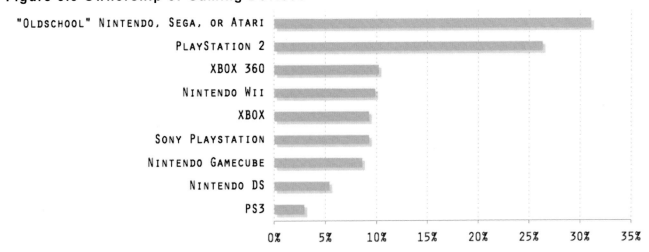

Gaming system ownership among respondents was demographically disproportionate, the gender divide in particular starkly apparent. Consistent with recent research into technology ownership and video game use, the younger male gamer archetype is confirmed by the current study. Male respondents 26 and under were much more likely to participate in gaming than older or female students. Table 5.2 shows that among respondents 27 and older, male-gendered respondents were twice as likely to own a gaming console or handheld, although 32% of female-gendered digital natives also reported owned gaming devices – a surprisingly high number. Digital immigrants were on average half as likely to own a gaming device, but were more gender equal in ownership than younger respondents. Older respondents and women were both more likely to own a Wii or Nintendo DS, reflecting national trends in gaming device consumption.

Table 5.2 Gaming Ownership by Gender and Status

	Gender	
	Male	**Female**
Native	68%	32%
Immigrant	27%	19%

5.2: Technology Use

Internet Engagement

A series of questions asked respondents to rate their levels of internet use and engagement. The largest share (32%) of respondents spent 11-20 hours using the internet in a typical week, while 21% spent 6-10 and 23% spent 21-30 hours online (Figure 5.4). Twenty percent of respondents reported spending more than 30 hours online on a weekly basis, with only 5% using the internet less than 5 hours per week during the same period. Eight percent of total respondents spent more than 40 hours online per week. When compared by age (Table 5.3), the division in internet use between graduates and undergraduates closely resembles the difference between digital natives and immigrant use. Contrary to assumptions that younger individuals spend more time online, higher age and academic status were both closely correlated with increased time spent online per week.

Figure 5.4 Weekly Internet Use

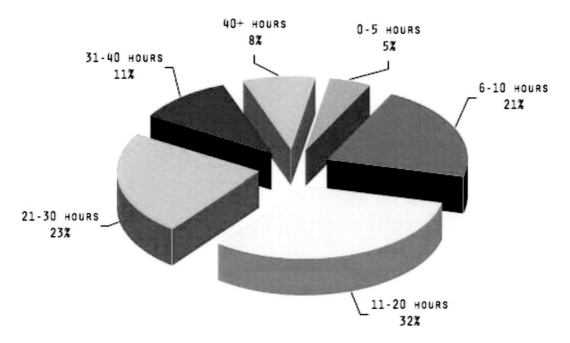

Table 5.3 illustrates that the greatest internet use differences among respondents of disparate digital and academic statuses is evident at the highest levels of engagement. Ohio University graduate students and digital immigrants were twice as likely to spend over 40 hours per week online than undergraduates or digital natives, who were most likely to spend 21-30 hours online. Four to five percent of all demographics averaged less than 5 hours online per week, while in general lower ranges of internet use were much more consistent between groups. That students 27 and older were likeliest to spend over 40 hours per week online supports research by the CIBER group questioning assumptions that "Google Generation" students are the heaviest internet users in a higher education context (2008).

Table 5.3 Weekly Internet Use by Digital and Academic Status

	Academic Status		Digital Status	
	Undergraduate	Graduate	Native	Immigrant
Less than 5 hours	4%	4%	5%	5%
6-10	22%	18%	22%	20%
11-20	33%	26%	32%	28%
21-30	23%	21%	23%	20%
31-40	10 %	15%	11%	12%
More than 40	7%	14%	8%	14%

Browser and Search Preferences

Survey 1 asked participants a series of questions on various aspects of their internet use habits. Approximately the same number of OU students reported a preference for Firefox or Internet Explorer (42.4% versus 42%), while 14% preferred the Mac-based Safari browser. This represents a notable departure from national web browser preferences for both Safari (3%) and Explorer (55%), but is typical of Firefox (41%) (Browser Statistics, 2008). Seventeen percent customized web browsers with extensions, AdBlocker, StumbleUpon and Google Toolbars among the most common. Eighty-seven percent listed Google as their preferred search engine, Yahoo second at 10%.

Google Use

Among Google products, 97% of students reported using Search, 60% Images, 50% Maps, 25% Gmail, 22% News, 21% Scholar, 10% Documents, and 8% Books, 5% used Talk, 5% Picasa, 3% blog search, and 2% Reader. Use of various Google products differed considerably by age (Table 5.4).

Table 5.4 Use of Google Products by Age

	17-19	20-22	23-26	27-30	31+
Search	98%	97%	95%	98%	99%
Images	66%	61%	54%	53%	37%
Maps	47%	51%	62%	55%	51%
News	21%	23%	21%	20%	23%
Gmail	17%	25%	44%	47%	34%
Scholar	13%	20%	38%	40%	37%
iGoogle	9%	9%	11%	11%	8%
Documents	8%	10%	15%	20%	20%
Books	5%	6%	14%	16%	11%
Talk	3%	4%	12%	12%	8%
Blog Search	2%	2%	4%	4%	6%
Picasa	2%	5%	13%	9%	8%
Reader	1%	2%	3%	6%	3%

While Search is used almost ubiquitously, older respondents used Scholar, Books and Documents more heavily. A larger proportion of younger students used Image search. Almost half of 27-30 year-olds use Gmail, and Google News is consistently used by about 22% of students in all age ranges.

Social Networking and Social Media

Respondents in Survey 1 also indicated their participation in social networking sites. Ninety percent of respondents used social software such as Facebook, MySpace, and/or Flickr. Eighty-six percent of total respondents used Facebook, 36% MySpace, 60% YouTube, 5% Flickr, 1% LinkedIn and/or Delicious. Numerous sites such as Orkut, Friendster, and Digg and were mentioned by respondents in the 'other' category, but not to a statistically significant extent. Whereas use of the social media technologies listed above was relatively consistent between genders, male students were more likely than female students *not* to use Facebook or MySpace by an almost 2:1 ratio, confirming research into disproportionate use of social networking sites by gender. Over 50% of Facebook users added 1-5 applications to their profiles, and among Facebook and MySpace users combined, over 50% posted comments to friends' profiles at least several times a week. Table 5.5 illustrates the use of social sites by age. Facebook was almost ubiquitously used by 17-22 year olds and while its use is inversely proportional to age, Facebook is still highly popular among Ohio University students under 30. MySpace was used by roughly 20-40% of students at all age ranges, with similarly higher use by younger demographics. Flickr was used most frequently by 27-30 year olds (21%), and only by 3% of 17-19 year olds. YouTube was used most heavily by the youngest respondents (67%), and least by 31+ year olds (25%). Less than one percent of all demographics used LinkedIn, and while delicious is little used in general, it is more likely to be accessed by older respondents. Older respondents were also more likely to indicate that they used a social technology not included on the questionnaire. Students 23 and older were twice as likely as 17-22 year olds to select 'other'.

Table 5.5 Use of Social Sites by Age

		17-19	20-22	23-26	27-30	31+
Facebook	Count	1171	1481	319	97	69
	% within age	94%	92%	76%	56%	35%
MySpace		493	585	152	58	38
		40%	36%	36%	34%	19%
Flickr		34	63	20	24	15
		3%	4%	5%	14%	8%
YouTube		833	1014	201	59	50
		67%	63%	48%	34%	25%
Delicious		7	13	7	3	6
		.6%	.8%	2%	2%	3%
LinkedIn		4	3	3	0	1
		.3%	.2%	.7%	0%	.5%
Other		40	57	31	9	13
		3%	4%	7%	5%	6%

Web Communication

Students in Survey 1 described their use of web-based communication tools and virtual environments. Sixteen percent of students used the web calling program Skype, another 1% used Tokbox, iChat, or another web calling client, while 22% of students had received a call via a similar service. Students who used web calling predominantly contacted friends/significant others (54%) and/or family (39%), while fewer reported calling instructors (3%) and/or businesses (3%), indicating that at the time of the survey web calling was used as a predominantly social communication medium. Eighty-six percent of survey respondents used IM, while 34% signed into their IM accounts using a web-based service such as Meebo. Thirty-four percent used application-based IM, and 18% were completely unfamiliar with web-based IM.

User-Generated Content and Virtual Worlds

Respondents were asked whether they used or produced content via several types of user-generated media. Thirty percent of students listened to podcasts regularly, whereas 8% did not know what a podcast was. Twelve percent of respondents reported posting to a personal blog, 4% maintained a website, and 3% had both a blog and a personal site. A greater proportion of students posted comments to blogs and online discussion forums than maintained them personally - 9% of students commented on blogs, 11% posted to online discussion forums, and 7% were active commenters on both blogs and forums. Eighteen percent of students read blogs at least once a week, 16% did so monthly, and 7% reported reading blogs on a daily basis. Surprisingly, 56% of students did not read blogs at all, although it is possible that a significant portion of these students incorrectly recognized blog-based pages as other types of content. Only 2% of students were totally unfamiliar with blogs. Of blog readers, 18% used a web-based feed reader (i.e. Google Reader), 2% used a browser-based reader (i.e. SageFeeds), 1% used a desktop aggregator (i.e. FeedDemon), and 44% reported not using any type of reader or aggregator. Surprisingly, fully 10% of students reported having edited a Wikipedia article, and a further 3% had edited or created an article in a different wiki. Fifty-five percent of students consulted wikis but did not edit them, and a much higher percentage of students were unfamiliar with wikis as a concept than those who were unfamiliar with blogs or podcasts - 16%. At the time of the survey, Twitter was only used by .3% of respondents and less than 1% of students regularly logged into Second Life (whereas 7% had done so more often at one point but had since decreased or discontinued their usage).

Knowledge of Emerging Technologies

Relative respondent unfamiliarity with specific emerging technologies is interesting to note. Figure 5.5 compares the percentage of students who indicated that they lacked knowledge of each emerging social tool surveyed, a frequent response choice in Survey 1 . Second Life was unknown to 35% of total participants, whereas blogs were unknown to only 2%. Although knowledge of Wikipedia itself was high, "wiki" was a term unfamiliar to close to 18% of the sample population. This indicates that Wikipedia may be seen as a unique service not necessarily representative of a category of web tool.

Figure 5.5 Relative Student Unfamiliarity with Emerging Technologies

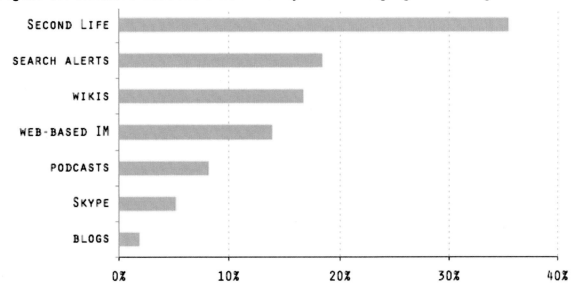

Social and Mobile Technology Use by Age

Distinct usage rates of emerging content and communication technologies are evident when respondents are segmented by age (Table 5.6) For example, only 29% of 17-19 year-olds listened occasionally or regularly to podcasts, whereas 41% of students aged 31 and older did so. If findings are representative of total campus usage rates, the number of students in each category in Table 5.6 represents roughly a quarter of the potential existing "market" for these technology services.

Table 5.6 Use of Emerging Technology Formats by Age

		Age of Respondent				
		17-19	20-22	23-26	27-30	31+
Web Calling	number of students	200	289	127	68	63
	% within age	16%	18%	31%	40%	33%
Second Life		57	126	48	17	19
		5%	8%	12%	10%	10%
Blogs		182	246	95	45	38
		15%	16%	23%	27%	20%
Web-based IM		875	1049	239	91	82
		71%	66%	59%	54%	43%
Podcasts		357	453	143	62	77
		29%	29%	35%	37%	41%
Text Messaging		1107	1349	275	98	97
		89%	85%	67%	58%	51%
Wikis		808	1119	303	122	147
		65%	71%	74%	73%	78%
Twitter		4	3	3	0	1
		.3%	.2%	.7%	0%	.5%

Figures indicate that older students were more likely to have used Second Life and wikis than younger students, although findings also show that basic knowledge of the term "wiki" may not have been as common among younger students. Text messaging was almost twice as common among younger students compared to older students, and web calling was by far the most popular among 27-30 year olds (this age range has the highest representation of graduate and international students at Ohio University, both recognized as heavy web calling user groups).

For purposes of accurate interpretation it should be noted that table 5.6 does not indicate frequency or recentness of use, only whether the participant had used the technology in the past. This is particularly significant in the case of Second Life, wherein other survey items indicated that overall student usage had decreased dramatically since the peak of the virtual world's popularity. The limitations of the online survey product used to create these surveys prevented more in-depth assessment of use frequency that would have been possible via multi-item question matrices like those featured in the revised sample survey instrument (Appendix A, Section D).

Academic Technologies

Survey 1 asked students to indicate how much of their online engagement was devoted to course-related activities. Roughly fifty percent of students reported spending half of their time online on course-related activities, while about a quarter of respondents spent 25%. The remaining students reported spending three quarters or more of their online time engaged in academics (Figure 5.6).

Figure 5.6 Time Online Spent on Academic Activities

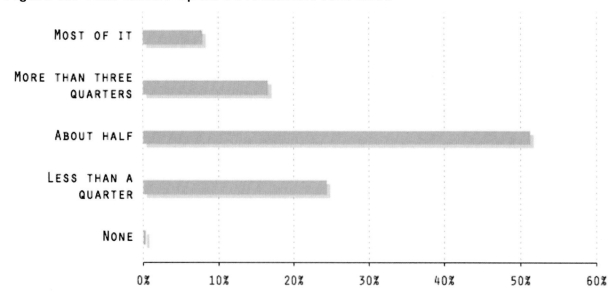

Table 5.7 indicates that graduate students and undergraduates spent different proportions of their online engaged in academic work, whereas digital immigrant and digital native populations were divided along very similar lines. Digital immigrants and graduate students were nearly three times as

likely as digital natives or undergraduate students to spend most of their online time engaged in academic tasks. The majority of undergraduates and digital immigrants spent about half or a quarter of their time online engaged in academic work.

Table 5.7 Time Online Spent on Academic Activities by Status

	Academic Status		Digital Status	
	Undergraduate	Graduate	Native	Immigrant
None	.2%	.5%	.2%	.5%
Less than a quarter	26%	17%	25%	17%
About half	54%	40%	53%	37%
More than three quarters	15%	24%	16%	25%
Most of it	5%	18%	6%	21%

Learning Management Systems and Course Blogs

Students responded to several items that gauged their use of the local LMS (Blackboard) as well as user-generated academic content and web-based coursework. Thirty-eight percent of students reported 75-100% of their classes had a presence in Blackboard, 32% reported that 50-75% did, 20% indicated that 25-50% of their classes used Blackboard, and the remaining 10% responded that only 0-25% were active in the LMS. Eighteen percent of survey participants had used a course-related blog while at Ohio University, and 25% reported taking a web-based course. Use of course blogs varied widely by discipline, and large numbers of students actually remained unsure whether they had used a blog in a classroom setting (Table 5.8).

Table 5.8 Use of Classroom Blogs by Major

	Yes	No	Unsure
Business	26%	64%	10%
Education	23%	64%	12%
Communications	22%	71%	7%
Humanities	19%	73%	8%
Undecided/Other	18%	74%	12%
Social Sciences	16%	77%	7%
Life/Health Sciences	14%	75%	11%
Fine Arts	13%	78%	9%
Engineering	12%	80%	8%
Physical Sciences	9%	84%	7%

Web-Based Tutorials

Respondents to Survey 1 described their use and perception of screencast tutorials, with sixteen percent using online tutorials in coursework at the university. When asked to rate features of online tutorials that they find effective, 55% of total respondents selected images and graphics, 39% indicated interactivity, 33% animation, 31% voice narration, 31% feedback, 29% quiz components, while 18% were unsure what features increase the effectiveness of online tutorials. Table 5.9 indicates that among those who rated at least one tutorial feature as effective, images and graphics were the most highly rated tutorial component by all age cohorts, with interactivity following at a considerable distance. Quizzes were rated the least effective learning component in general. Variations in preferred tutorial features are evident among students of different age ranges. Younger students were more likely to find quiz components valuable, whereas older students were more likely to value interactivity.

Table 5.9 Receptivity to Tutorial Features by Age

	17-19	20-22	23-26	27-30	31+
Audio narration	47%	48%	53%	46%	52%
Images and graphics	85%	87%	89%	85%	88%
Interactivity	60%	60%	66%	65%	69%
Animation	53%	49%	54%	64%	49%
Feedback	49%	50%	42%	50%	46%
Quizzes	51%	44%	38%	43%	38%

These age-based differences run somewhat counter to the common assumption that digital natives are inherently more experiential and multimedia-based learners. That said, it should be noted that findings relating to tutorial features describe differences in respondent self-perception rather than actual demonstrated learning effectiveness.

5.3: Technology Skill

Survey participants were asked to rate their skill levels in a variety of computing and research tasks on a Likert scale (1 = not at all skilled, 5 = very skilled). Students were most confident in their abilities to use word processing software such as Microsoft Word, closely followed by using Blackboard for coursework – students felt they were highly skilled in these areas (Figure 5.7). Respondents rated themselves somewhat less skilled using presentation software such as Microsoft PowerPoint. Research options fared similarly – students rated their ability to find books and articles for assignments as well as their skill using library resources for research as moderate (see Chapter 6.3 for more detailed treatment of library and research skill self-assessment).

Figure 5.7 Self-Assessment of Library, Research, and Technology Skills

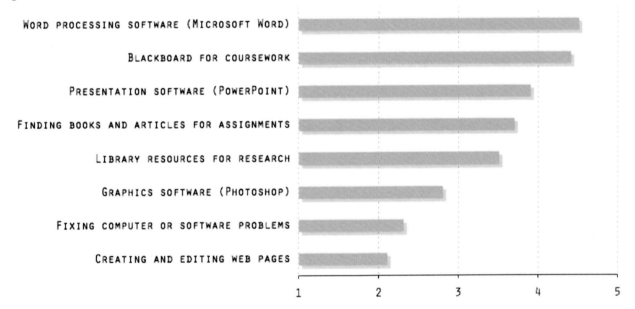

Students were less confident using graphics software such as Photoshop, fixing computer software or hardware problems, and/or editing web pages. Engineering majors were most self-assured of all students in their computing abilities, but had among the lowest self-assessment of library and research skills (for more discussion of library and research skills see Chapter 6.3). When all categories of technology self-assessment are combined, digital natives were somewhat more likely to rate their skill levels as average than digital immigrants (60% vs. 51%), whereas digital immigrants are more likely to rate their technology skills at low (20% vs. 15%) and high (30% vs. 26%) levels than digital natives.

5.4: Technology Adoption

When asked to identify with a range of statements that described how quickly they tended to use new computing and communication tools, 46% of students selected, "I adopt new technologies at about the same time everyone else does," 25% indicated that they "generally take a while to use new technologies," another 25% responded that "I tend to use new technologies somewhat before other people do," 5% "adopt new technologies before anyone else," and 2% "avoid using new technologies whenever possible" (Figure 5.8). According to Everett Rogers' standard scale of technology adoption, 30% of Ohio University students can therefore be considered "innovators" or early adopters, 46% mainstream adopters, and 27% late adopters. These figures depart significantly from national trends reported in the 2007 ECAR Study of Undergraduates and Information Technology, wherein only 13% of participants identified themselves as late technology adopters. Technology adoption by major is indicative of significant differences in the sample population (Table 5.10). Students in Business, Engineering, and Communications were more inclined to view themselves as early adopters, whereas respondents associated with Fine Arts, Humanities, and the Life/Health Sciences were likelier to self-identify as late adopters. Curiously, students in the Life/Health Sciences were the least likely to consider themselves early adopters.

Figure 5.8 Rates of Technology Adoption

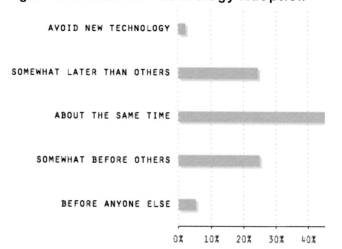

Table 5.10 Technology Adoption by Major

	Business	Communications	Education	Engineering	Fine Arts	Humanities	Life/Health Sciences	Physical Sciences	Social Sciences
Late	14%	17%	28%	15%	32%	35%	33%	28%	30%
Mainstream	55%	50%	52%	37%	39%	41%	48%	46%	48%
Early	32%	33%	20%	48%	29%	24%	19%	27%	23%

When segmented by digital status, respondents born before 1981 were more likely to view themselves as average or late technology adopters, whereas respondents born after 1981 were more likely to identify as average or early adopters (Figure 5.9). Digital natives were much more likely to view themselves as average or mainstream technology adopters.

Figure 5.9 Technology Adoption by Digital Status

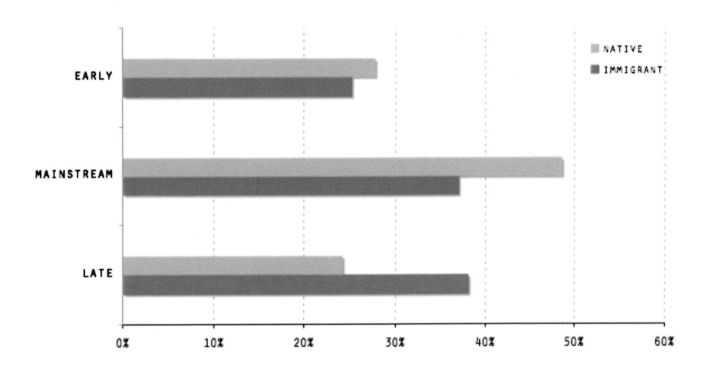

Figure 5.9 reveals deep differences in self-perception of technology adoption among older and younger respondents. Considering that higher actual usage and ownership rates of mobile, gaming, computing, and social tools among younger students are consistently apparent, this data tends to affirm the theory that younger students have a different view of what comprises "technology" than older respondents. In the words of Alan Kay, each generation experiences a phenomenon wherein "technology is only technology if it was invented after they were born" (cited in Prensky, 2000, p. 38).

It is likely that although their communication, computing and social tool usage and ownership rates are generally higher, young students are more apt to view themselves as average in comparison to their peers in terms of how they use these tools, and therefore report modest adoption patterns. Older respondents less likely to view themselves as average in terms of technology adoption in part because they may associate "new" tools and devices with a degree of learning or behavioral change that they believe younger generations consider routine.

Chapter 6: Student Library Cultures

A second goal of the Student Technology Survey was to create an accurate and insightful portrayal of the library culture of Ohio University students, which I define as consisting of student attitudes, perceptions, needs, and expectations in respect to library facilities and information resources. Described here as the overall Student Library Profile, this information is presented in four sections: 6.1 Use, 6.2 Perceptions, 6.3 Skill, and 6.4 Technology Receptivity.

6.1: Library Use

Survey results revealed a student population consistently engaged with the Ohio University Libraries, although somewhat more so with its physical than its electronic facilities. Seventy-five percent of respondents visited Alden Library on at least a weekly basis, while 11% did so daily. Online resources were accessed less frequently - 61% of participants made at least a weekly visit to the library website, while 9% used the site on a daily basis. More respondents infrequently or never used the library website relative to those that report never visiting library facilities - 11% versus 3%, respectively (Figure 6.1).

Figure 6.1 Library Facility and Website Use

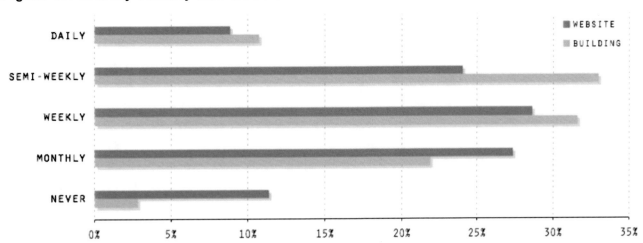

When asked what tasks they typically engage in when visiting the library website, 71% of students indicated that they searched for books and journals, 62% searched for articles in a library-provided database, and 42% used InfoTree, the Libraries' online subject resource portal (Figure 6.2).

Figure 6.2 Library Website Use

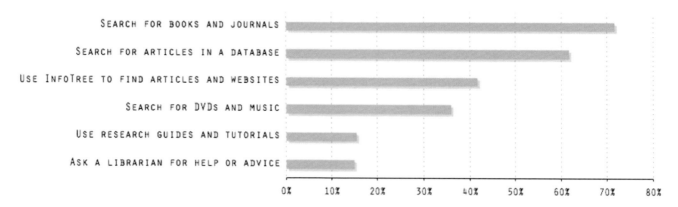

A further 36% searched the library website for DVDs and music, 15% used research guides or tutorials, and 15% asked a librarian for assistance. Undergraduate and graduate students used online and physical library facilities at different rates and for different purposes. Figure 6.3 shows that while graduate students accessed the library website, building, and computers somewhat more frequently on average than undergraduates, they were considerably more likely to be heavy users of the library website.

Figure 6.3 Library Website, Facility, and Computer Use by Academic Status

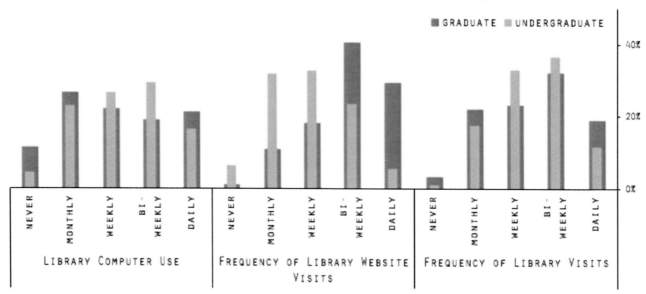

It is interesting to note that although access rates differ, task-based library website use was remarkably consistent between graduate and undergraduate students (Table 6.1). Article searching emerged as the most common task, followed by DVD/media searching. Use of research guides, tutorials, and Ask a Librarian options was consistently modest for both undergraduates and graduates.

Table 6.1 Typical Library Website Use by Academic Status

	Undergraduate	Graduate
Search for books and journals	36%	37%
Search for articles in a database	72%	69%
Search for DVDs and music	62%	58%
Use InfoTree to find articles and websites	41%	44%
Use research guides and tutorials	15%	17%
Ask a librarian for help or advice	15%	16%

Building Use

When visiting Alden Library in person, respondents were on average most likely to use library computers on at least a weekly basis, whereas they tended to engage in assignment-related research, search for items in the library catalog, or use article databases less frequently. Asking a librarian for help with an assignment, checking out library materials, and using the library café (Café Bibliotech) tended to occur the least frequently (on approximately a monthly basis). Thirty-five percent of respondents used library computers more than once a week. When using library computers, students most frequently conducted research for assignments, consulted the library website, accessed presentation software (Microsoft PowerPoint), or used Blackboard (Table 6.2).

Table 6.2 Weekly Library Computer Use by Academic Status

	Undergraduate	Graduate
Research for assignments	54%	47%
Use Blackboard	26%	34%
Use Facebook or MySpace	27%	23%
Use Graphics software	27%	27%
Use Presentation software	47%	44%
Use Word processing software	28%	28%
Access library website	46%	37%
Use email	24%	29%
Use IM	13%	8%

Building Use by Major

Students in the Humanities, Social Sciences, and Business tended to visit the library more frequently than other majors, whereas Science and Engineering students used the library somewhat less frequently (Figure 6.4). Life and Health Science students were the least likely to visit the physical library, whereas students in the Social Sciences and Humanities were the most frequent daily visitors. Students in all disciplines were most likely to visit the library weekly or several times a week.

Figure 6.4 Library Visits by Major

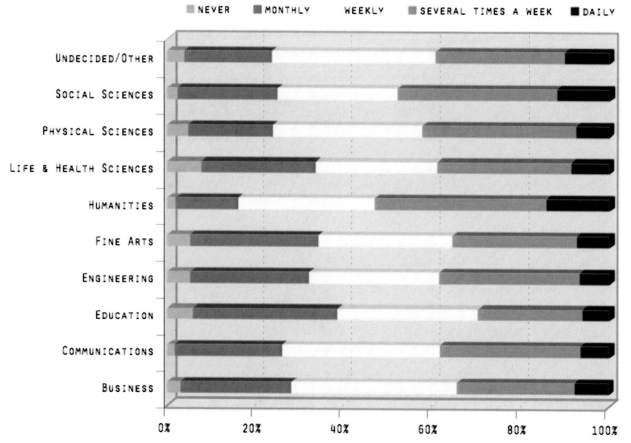

Library building and website use suggests that a visit to a physical facility does not necessarily coincide with the utilization of online or print library resources, which confirms research indicating that library buildings are used for social and academic purposes by students (Lippincott, 2005). It also speaks to the ways in which students typically utilize print and electronic library resources, usually on a point-of-need basis relative to more consistent types of facility use such as computing or group study. The disproportionate number of students that report rarely or never using online library resources relative to physical facilities indicates that many may turn to external web-based resources to conduct research, which may at times unknowingly lead them to library-sponsored content (21% of students indicated that they use Google Scholar, for example, which is linked to OhioLINK journal content on campus). Whether these students infrequently receive research-based assignments and/or are unfamiliar with library resources merits closer consideration. Overall, online access frequency of library tools at OU should not be read as insignificant. That well over half of respondents visit the library website at least once a week is an indication of positive library web engagement. Graduate students tend to be heavier users of the library website, indicative of higher average information needs in terms of academic research.

6.2: Library Perceptions

Figure 6.5 Library v. Web Information Resources

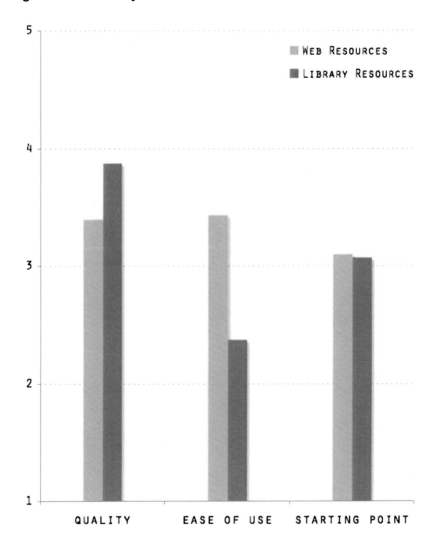

When students rated online library resources against general web resources, distinct patterns emerged that mirror recent research into student perceptions of library-provided vs. web-accessible information (OCLC, 2005). Participants consistently evaluated library resources such as article databases, the library website, and the ALICE catalog highly in terms of their information quality, but lacking in ease of use and suitability for the beginning stages of academic research (Figure 6.5). Sources such as Google and Wikipedia received high overall ratings for ease of use and suitability for beginning research, but fared poorly in terms of their information quality (Figure 6.6). On 1-5 respective Likert scales for gauging quality, ease of use, and suitability for starting research. Web-based library resources consistently received average ratings for ease of use, much lower than general web resources. The OU campus website received the lowest ratings of all sites and information sources surveyed. Graduate students rated library-sponsored resources more positively than undergraduates. These findings closely mirror similar items in the 2006 OCLC report, College Students' Perceptions of Libraries and Information Resources.

Library Evaluation

Virtually all participants responded to three optional items in Survey 2 that invited them to provide open-ended positive, negative, and general feedback regarding the OU Libraries. The 1,651 participants in Survey 2 submitted a total of 4,198 discrete, substantive responses to these items, which were coded, analyzed, and grouped into positive and negative comments related to four areas:

Buildings, Technology, Services, and Resources (Figure 6.7). Responses consisting of nonspecific satisfaction or dissatisfaction were counted separately. Two hundred and seventy six participants offered general praise or appreciation in response to the first open-ended item, which asked them to list the OU Libraries' best aspect. One hundred and seventy three indicated that they had no specific

Figure 6.6 Rating Library and Web Information Resources

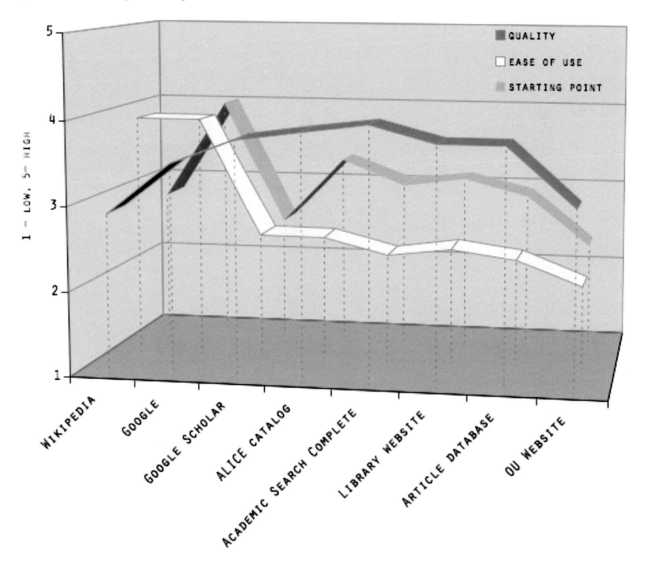

criticism in response to the second open-ended item, which invited users to list the Libraries' worst aspect (whereas the item that asked respondents to explain the OU Libraries' best aspect was almost ubiquitously answered). Seven hundred and eighty one respondents declined to provide further feedback on the third open-ended item, which invited their additional comments. Figure 6.7 illustrates the frequency breakdown of combined positive and negative open-ended responses by category. Generally, Services and Resources emerge as the most commonly praised features, whereas Buildings and Technology were more frequently criticized.

Figure 6.7 Positive and Negative Feedback by Category

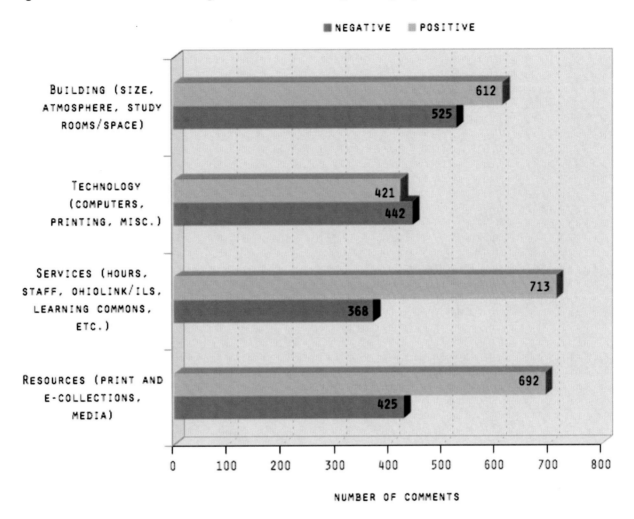

■ NEGATIVE ■ POSITIVE

BUILDING (SIZE, ATMOSPHERE, STUDY ROOMS/SPACE)
612
525

TECHNOLOGY (COMPUTERS, PRINTING, MISC.)
421
442

SERVICES (HOURS, STAFF, OHIOLINK/ILS, LEARNING COMMONS, ETC.)
713
368

RESOURCES (PRINT AND E-COLLECTIONS, MEDIA)
692
425

0   100   200   300   400   500   600   700   800

NUMBER OF COMMENTS

Via these three open-ended items, students expressed a wide range of opinions and suggestions regarding library facilities, services, staff, resources, and technology. Among the many items flagged for improvement, the lack of sufficient library computing, the need for longer hours on all floors, general enhancements to the building, more capable and friendlier student staff, and consistent enforcement of quiet areas emerged as priorities (Figure 6.8). In regards to print and electronic collections, respondents indicated that they valued library resources but wished that they were organized in a more straightforward fashion. They desired more comfortable amenities in addition to increased collaborative and quiet individualized study space within the main library. Many described the library website as "confusing" and difficult to use, and requested either a redesign or a superior way to perform article and book searching. Curiously, many participants seemed to associate some measure of responsibility for the main campus website with the Libraries, frequently asking us to improve its poor navigation and search functions.

Figure 6.8 Negative Perceptions of the Ohio University Libraries

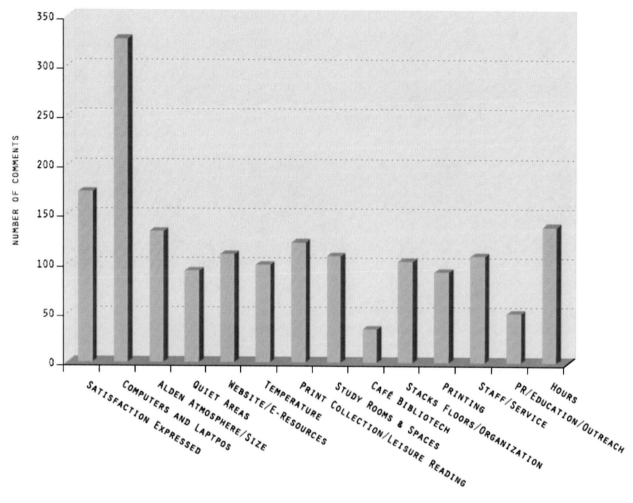

Students named many of the same features as the most positive aspects of the OU Libraries, including library computing (Figure 6.9), building atmosphere and quiet areas, extended hours, study rooms, print collections, electronic articles, and general resources. Many Learning Commons services were positively identified (e.g., laptop checkouts, Student Writing Center, extended hours, Media Library) and the Learning Commons floor itself was often referred to by name. Respondents regularly praised consortial OhioLINK and intercampus borrowing, citing the availability of textbooks as a highly appreciated service. Professional and classified library staff were consistently praised as helpful and knowledgeable, and in a strikingly consistent dichotomy, student workers were routinely criticized for their lack of knowledge and poor public service skills. That respondents so consistently distinguished between "librarians" and students on the basis of service quality is noteworthy, and supports recent research into staffing makeup and service effectiveness (Fitzpatrick, Moore, & Lang, 2008). If these findings are even moderately representative of general perceptions of student versus professional service quality, they findings merit closer investigation in order to better inform the ongoing debate over information and reference point deprofessionalization.

Figure 6.9 Positive Perceptions of the Ohio University Libraries

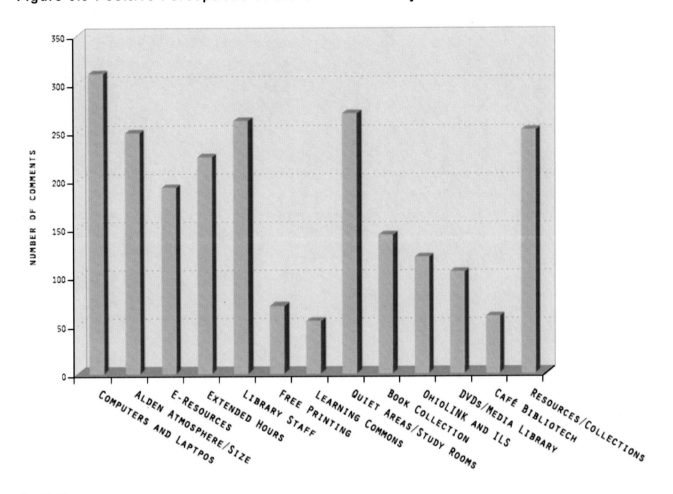

Buildings

In regards to physical library facilities, students expressed an unequivocal desire for longer hours and more group and individual study space. The character of the request for extended hours differed by academic status; graduates more often desired earlier weekend opening times, whereas undergraduates wanted more floors open 24 hours. A roughly equivalent number of students stated a need for quiet individual study space as collaborative study areas, indicating that Alden Library's tiered floor approach (degreed collaborative and quiet areas designated by floor) is effective but not sufficient to meet campus demand. Students appreciated the overall gestalt of the library and frequently cited its "atmosphere" as positive motivation to study. They also reported that updated fixtures, furnishings, and amenities would be much appreciated, particularly on the stacks floors. The phrase "more comfy seats" was most common among building-related suggestions.

Services

Respondents were overwhelmingly appreciative of a wide range of library services, including but not limited to face-to-face interactions with library staff, OhioLINK/ILS/intercampus borrowing, and extended building hours. Students were twice as likely to praise library services as they were to criticize them, by far the most positive praise to critique ratio of all categories. Longer hours on all floors and earlier weekend opening times emerged as respective priorities of undergraduates and graduate students. As previously stated, respondents often expressed an explicit desire for better trained, friendlier, and more capable student workers on service desks.

Resources

Unexpectedly, a major finding of this study concerns the strong and unsolicited undergraduate and graduate student desire for improved access to print reading material, which contradicts a common assumption that newer cohorts of learners are increasingly uninterested in traditional modes of literacy. When asked to critique one aspect of library services and/or to offer general commentary on the OU Libraries, a surprisingly large percentage of students across all demographic groups requested an expanded leisure reading area, "more fiction," more textbooks, a generally updated print collection, and/or a greater range of readily accessible new books.

Many specifically indicated that they would like to be able to more easily browse fiction books for leisure or relaxation (roughly 15% of total student comments to the general open-ended question). Dissatisfaction with physical and digital collection arrangement was similarly widespread. Users routinely described Alden's stacks floors as "confusing" and "creepy," and characterized the library website in similarly critical terms.

Library Awareness

A similar student library and technology study at the University of Michigan Libraries asked users to indicate whether they thought the library offered a variety of services, all of which were actually available at the time of the survey (Chapman, et al., 2007). Students at Michigan were most aware of a number of electronic resources, including the library website, electronic articles, and article databases. Relatively well known were several Ask a Librarian and library outreach options, while among the least known services were subject research guides, software classes, office material delivery, and IM reference. A similar item was included in Survey 2 in to test student awareness of library services (Figure 6.10). Percentages in figure 6.10 indicate the number of respondents in Survey 2 who believed the OU Libraries currently offer each service.

While accurate comparison of the two surveys is difficult due to differences in sample size and administration conditions, it is interesting to note the ways in which responses differed by institution. Students at Ohio University tended to be most aware of Learning Commons services such as group study rooms, DVD checkouts, and in-person assistance from a librarian, whereas digital services had a consistently higher profile at Michigan, Ohio University student awareness of library-sponsored electronic articles was also quite high - roughly 95% of respondents were aware than the library provides full-text articles online. The same did not hold true for electronic books, however.

Figure 6.10 Awareness of Library Services

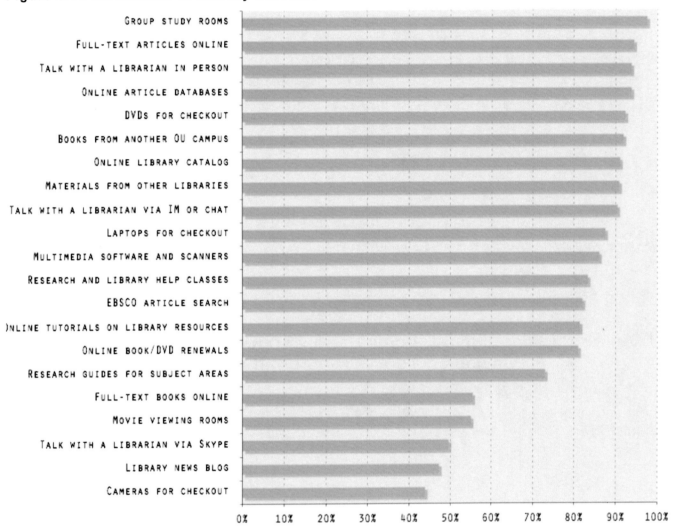

In both the Michigan and Ohio surveys only about half of respondents were aware that the library provided full-text e-books, which supports recent research indicating dismal student awareness of electronic books on an international scale ("Survey finds", 2008). High student awareness of IM reference at Ohio University is an item of considerable departure from the Michigan study, wherein IM reference was among the least known services. Areas that received relatively high recognition at OU included library classes, online material renewals, and subject guides. In addition to e-books, other little known local services included the library news blog, movie viewing rooms, cameras for checkout, and the pilot "Skype a Librarian" service, which had only existed for a short time when the survey was conducted.

Library Outreach

The item that tested student awareness of existing library services was intentionally placed near the end of Survey 2, directly before the final open-ended question that allowed students to submit additional commentary or suggestions. An unexpectedly large number of students indicated their surprise at the range of options they were not aware of prior to the survey, and a large number indicated their desire to more fully understand library programs and services. A surprising proportion of respondents made direct requests for the Libraries to provide more outreach, PR, and user education, stating that participation in the survey itself had been an important learning experience. This unintended but welcome outcome of the scan was frequently reflected in student verbatim comments:

Do surveys like these that keep the students up to date and remind students of the different things the library offers.

get more surveys in [sic] with better publicity among on-campus students need more publicity about services offered because many students are not aware they are available.

the library should publicize what it has to offer.

As a first year student, I didn't really know how useful Alden can be. Obviously it's a library, but it offers way more than that.

If there were an e-mail list, I would sign up for it… it would be nice to find out via e-mail, rather than when I have to use the bathroom.

If more people knew how good of a resource the library was, i [sic] think more people would use it … Stigma about being a dork if you go there would be reduced.

I like the library and what it has to offer, I just wish that I knew more when I was a freshman.

6.3: Library Skill

Reported levels of technology skill (word processing, computer troubleshooting, etc.) were relatively consistent among students of different academic statuses, whereas self-assessment of research skills (locating books and articles, using library resources) by graduates and undergraduates was markedly different (Figure 6.11). While it is not advisable to interpret student self-assessment as evidence of actual skill, these figures may be understood as gauging relative confidence and/or comfort with the resources in question. Graduate students were likelier to report high general skill levels in technology and were significantly more confident in their information-seeking abilities than undergraduates. However, slightly more graduate students reported low technology skills than undergraduates, who typically rated both their library and technology skills as average. Undergraduates were twice as likely to characterize their research skills as moderate to poor.

Figure 6.11 Self-Assessment of Overall Research and Technology Skills

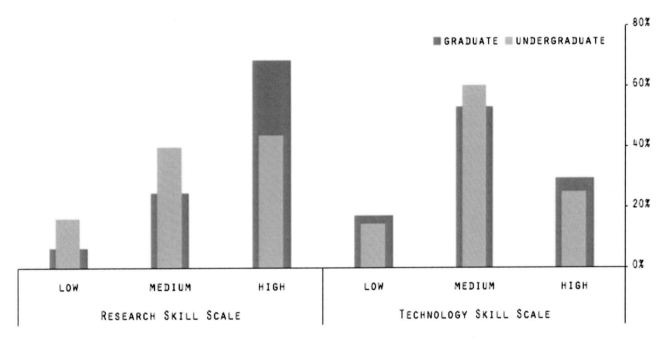

It is interesting to note that on average, on a 1-5 Likert scale, students rated themselves almost equivalently skilled at "finding books and articles for assignments" and "using library resources for research" (3.7 vs. 3.5), similar response choices phrased to offer insight into student perceptions of the library's role in the research process. Despite this initial similarity, when each category is unpacked significant differences become that suggest library-related tasks may be perceived as distinct from and potentially more difficult than other aspects of research. This disparity is illustrated by Figure 6.12, which depicts differences in self-perceptions of general research skills in comparison to library-specific research skills. Significantly more respondents rated themselves the most skilled at general research ("finding books and articles for assignments") versus library-specific research ("using library resources for research").

Figure 6.12 Self-Assessment of General and Library-Specific Research Skills

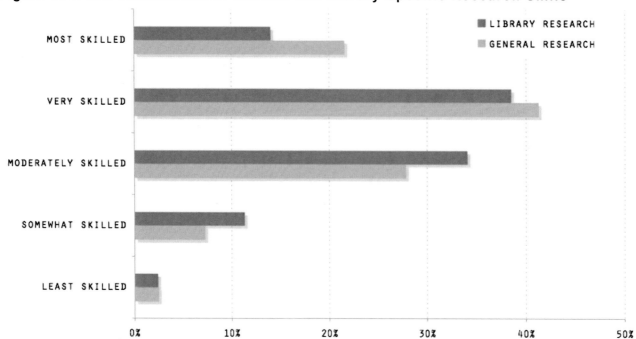

Among different academic majors, self-perception of research skill is quite distinct (Table 6.3). Students from disciplines that represent the heaviest library usage such as Fine Arts and Social Sciences, and Humanities were most likely to view themselves as very skilled at finding books and articles as well as using library resources for research. In general, Business and Science majors were least confident in their research and skills.

Table 6.3 Self-Assessment of General Research Skills by Academic Discipline

	Business	Communications	Education	Engineering	Fine Arts	Humanities	Life/Health Sciences	Physical Sciences	Social Sciences
Least skilled	2%	2%	5%	3%	2%	2%	3%	2%	2%
Somewhat skilled	8%	6%	7%	6%	5%	5%	8%	8%	8%
Moderately skilled	35%	26%	26%	31%	27%	19%	31%	29%	22%
Very skilled	42%	44%	43%	39%	37%	38%	39%	42%	44%
Most skilled	13%	22%	19%	21%	30%	36%	20%	19%	25%

6.4: Library Technology Receptivity

A number of items in Survey 1 asked respondents to indicate their interest in a number of emerging mobile and social library technology tools, contextualized in each instance by concrete descriptions of tasks and functions (i.e., texting call numbers, calling a librarian via Skype). In effect, students were responding to items that asked if they would be likely to use emerging platforms to accomplish specific library and research-related tasks. Table 6.4 compares student receptiveness to emerging library technologies by digital status and academic status. The range of receptivity represented in this table was computed by averaging a series of similarly-scaled items rating potential student use of a variety of future or existing library services such as web calling, text messaging, mobile browsing, toolbar extensions, and social networking sites on a scale of low, potential, and high interest (not including Blackboard library services).

Findings indicate that in general, older students and/or graduate students at Ohio University demonstrated higher interest levels in emerging technology services, complicating the common assumption that younger users will be more receptive to library services offered via new and social tools based on their higher relative use and adoption levels of these tools in a non-library setting. This also challenges the notion that older students prefer more "traditional" modes of access and assistance by virtue of their generational affiliation. When overall respondent interest in this series of mobile and social library tools is averaged, receptivity to emerging library technologies by both digital immigrants and graduate students was significantly higher than that of digital natives and undergraduates. Surprisingly, according to Table 6.4, the most technologically receptive respondents overall are students 27 years of age and older, 42% of whom expressed strong interest in a series of mobile and social library tools (relative to 23% of respondents 26 and younger). This difference is far less marked between graduate and undergraduate students (33% vs. 23%, respectively), indicating that among survey participants, increased age was a stronger indicator than graduate status (and by extension, information need) in determining interest in social and mobile library tools.

Table 6.4 Receptivity to New Library Technologies by Digital/Academic Status

	Digital Status		Academic Status	
	Native	Immigrant	Undergraduate	Graduate
Not receptive	24%	11%	24%	22%
Somewhat receptive	53%	47%	53%	45%
Very receptive	23%	42%	23%	33%

Although digital immigrants and graduate students are most receptive overall to the range of emerging library services surveyed, there is considerable variation in receptivity among different demographics based the type of technology in question (i.e., social vs. mobile vs. academic).

Respondent receptivity to library technologies by type is summarized below, followed by a closer analysis of trends and implications in Chapter 7.

Social Software

When asked whether they would use a library search or Ask a Librarian application in Facebook, 38% of Facebook users reported that they would, 30% would not, and 32% indicated potential interest. Open-ended responses to this question reveal that student opinion is highly polarized on the subject of a library presence in Facebook (see verbatim comments). About half of respondents indicated that a Facebook application would be useful because of the amount of time they spend logged into the site during the course of the day. In the words of one student, "it would be convenient. If I already had the Facebook site up I could search for things at the same time." The other half indicated that existing library services were sufficient and/or that Facebook is desirably separate from school activities, clearly reflecting the "creepy treehouse" or unwanted social site colonization effect. Facebook library applications received their highest overall receptivity rankings by 1st and 5th-year undergraduates, although older and more frequent library users were also likely to value library viability in Facebook.

Selected Verbatim Comments - Library Facebook Applications

Sounds convenient and interesting...I hope it's simple.

... It is a good source to use if you have something on facebook that both gets into the social world and academic world

seems weird and complicated

I am on facebook 24/7 and if i [sic] had something on there like an app from our school's library, i think it would help me go to the library and take out books and music. just help me expand my knowledge of literature.

That would kick ass.

Why encourage people to have less social interaction as well as spend more time on Facebook. Are you trying to put librarians out of a job? Who came up with this idea? They should be the first one replaced by a Facebook application!

it would be an easier transition from my social online activities to actually doing homework.

sometimes facebook applications are really slow, i [sic] may just use the actual library website which could be more reliable

You can already IM the librarian and applications on Facebook just clutter your page.

Facebook is just something for fun. I think it might ruin it if there were homework help applications added.

When asked the same question regarding library applications in MySpace, current and former users of the site responded in a radically different way. Only 8% of users reported that they would benefit from such an application, while 68% indicated that they would not and 24% remained unsure. In the open-ended commentary, students overwhelmingly expressed disdain for MySpace as a social networking site rather than for the idea of a social library application or profile itself (see verbatim comments). Most indicated that they simply no longer used MySpace, or had come to rely on it exclusively for music information. In the words of two respondents, "I wouldn't touch MySpace if you paid me," and" I only use MySpace for music."

Selected Verbatim Comments - Library MySpace Applications

It could be useful, especially if they sent out messages and bullitins [sic] about special events or services.

I don't view My Space as being as secure as other websites.

I hate MySpace.

I have a MySpace account, but do not use it as frequently as Facebook, thus I am unsure if I would use the MySpace add-on.

I find the OU Library website and searches to be adequate.

It would be easier for me because some times finding the Library site and navigating the site can be a little hard.

MySpace kind of sucks now

Myspace is not related to education whereas facebook is.

myspace is a joke...it takes to long and is full of weirdoes. (no one uses it anymore because there is no privacy on myspace)

Browser Customization

Among emerging technology formats surveyed, toolbar customization received the most positive response from students overall. A large proportion of respondents expressed definite or potential interest in a downloadable library search and information help toolbar in Firefox or Explorer. Seventy-nine percent indicated that they were definitely or potentially likely to use a library toolbar, while only 28% were not likely to do so. Early indications from a library browser toolbar pilot program at Ohio University confirm these findings among faculty, as well (Wilson, in press).

Texting, Mobile Browsing, and Internet Communication

Forty-four percent of respondents who send text messages from their mobile phones reported definite or potential interest in SMS library services, while 56% were uninterested. When asked to rate specific texting services, 38% indicated interest in renewing books or DVDs via text, 35% wanted to receive overdue notifications or other account information, 28% would be likely to send call numbers and titles from the online catalog, and 21% would ask a librarian for help, while 10% were not interested in any of these options. Fourteen percent of total respondents reported they would definitely access library resources via the mobile web, while 54% were uninterested and 31% were unsure. Thirty-seven percent of students expressed strong or potential interested in contacting a librarian via Skype or another web calling service, while 64% were uninterested.

Blackboard Services

Library integration within Blackboard received the most enthusiastic support of all potential web-based library technologies included in the survey, far surpassing all other areas of library technology development with the exception of web browser customization. When asked what library services they would be likely to use in Blackboard, 65% of students indicated that an online catalog search function would be useful. Sixty-two percent desired an article search function, and 38% expressed interest in some type of Ask a Librarian service in Blackboard (Figure 6.13). Less popular options included chat hours for research help from subject specialists (26%) and library tutorials (22%). Only 15% indicated that none of the above options would be useful to them in Blackboard.

Figure 6.13 Preferred Blackboard Library Services

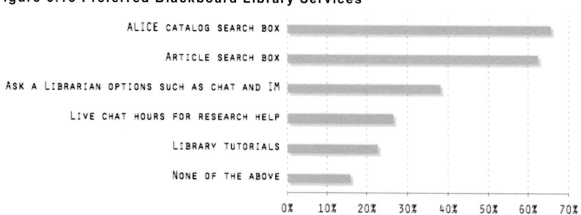

Graduate and undergraduate students were relatively consistent in their interest in library services in Blackboard. Table 6.5 indicates that undergraduates were much more receptive to Ask a Librarian options in Blackboard (40% vs. 29%), whereas graduate students are somewhat less likely to consider no Blackboard options useful (19% vs. 15%). Graduates were only slightly more interested in an article search box in Blackboard (65%) than undergraduates (61%). These academic status disparities are likely due to different rates of LMS use in graduate and undergraduate classes.

Table 6.5 Receptivity to Blackboard Services by Academic Status

	Undergraduate	Graduate
Ask a Librarian options (chat, IM)	40%	29%
ALICE catalog search box	66%	62%
Article search box	61%	65%
Live chat hours for research help	27%	26%
Library tutorials	23%	21%
None of the above	15%	19%

Library Technology Receptivity by Major

Trends in receptivity to library technologies by academic major were consistent with other self-assessment findings. Table 6.6 shows students from each academic discipline that indicated either definite or potential interest in emerging technology types. Students from library-intensive disciplines such as Fine Arts, Humanities, and the Social Sciences were generally more receptive to new technologies in a library context, even though they are not the heaviest technology users or earliest technology adopters overall.

Notable exceptions to this trend exist, however. Business and Engineering students were considerably more likely to be receptive to mobile browsing library services, whereas students in Education are among the most interested in browser toolbars. Communications students were more inclined towards library Facebook applications, while Engineering majors were the most receptive of all respondents to web calling library services. Students in the Physical Sciences expressed the most support for library text messaging services, closely followed by the Humanities and Life/Health Sciences.

Table 6.6 Receptivity to Emerging Library Services by Major

	Business	Communications	Education	Engineering	Fine Arts	Humanities	Life/Health Sciences	Physical Sciences	Social Sciences
Facebook	61%	67%	61%	51%	68%	59%	55%	56%	62%
MySpace	18%	18%	26%	19%	27%	19%	19%	17%	23%
Browser toolbars	74%	78%	83%	70%	81%	84%	79%	73%	77%
Text messaging	70%	69%	69%	65%	68%	74%	72%	75%	69%
Mobile browsing	27%	20%	17%	28%	23%	17%	19%	19%	19%
Web calling	37%	32%	40%	46%	38%	41%	33%	36%	34%
Blackboard	62%	69%	71%	57%	73%	71%	60%	62%	67%

Chapter 7: Trends in Technology Receptivity

A number of trends among Ohio University students emerge in Chapters 5 and 6, yet it is challenging to determine clear patterns in respondent interest in "Library 2.0" services based solely on technology type or application. Figure 7.1 compares self-reported use probabilities of six emerging library tools. This figure, which reflects weighted relative receptivity by the total sample population of Survey 1 to a series of specific library tools, clearly illustrates that student library technology receptivity varies widely by both technology application (e.g. mobile vs. social) and brand distinction within similar technology categories (e.g. Facebook vs. MySpace).

Figure 7.1 Relative Interest in Specific Library Technologies

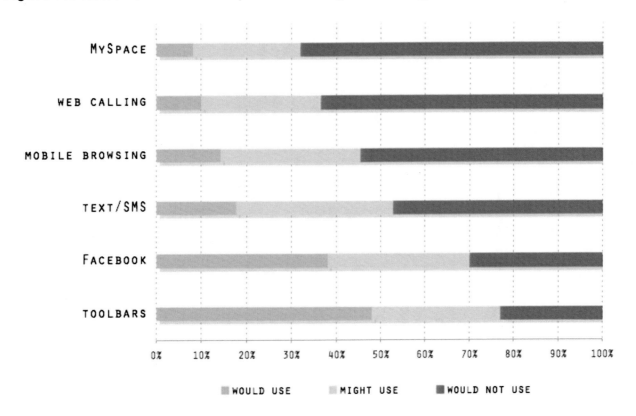

According to Figure 7.1, among the mobile and social tools identified by the Technology Team as promising for future development, respondents were most likely to anticipate using downloadable toolbars in Firefox and/or Facebook library applications. MySpace was almost uniformly panned in a library context as well as for social use, although older users were likelier to report receptivity to library MySpace integration. Disruptive library tools such as texting, mobile browsing, and web calling were perceived as very usable in a library service setting by a smaller proportion of respondents, and potentially usable by a larger proportion of respondents. In the case of mobile browsing and web calling, at the time of the survey both commanded a small marketshare relative to more established telephony and web access methods, but each is likely to become more viable as a library service as the technologies upon which they are based grow more sophisticated and widely adopted. These relatively well-received tools stand in contrast to MySpace, which exemplifies the risk inherent in library technology obsolescence. Clearly, disinterest in MySpace library applications reveals that the "shelf life" of social and mobile technologies has a large effect on their perceived utility in a library context. In addition, the dynamic nature of technology disruption dictates that now, only a year after the original study was conducted, Figure 7.1 would likely look quite different. This is due in large part to the continued rise of Facebook and increased diffusion of mobile internet use due to the popularity of the iPhone and its resulting competition.

Table 7.1 Relative and Absolute Library Technology Receptivity by Academic Status

		Undergraduate	Graduate	Total
Facebook	number of students	1937	248	2185
	% within ac. status	66%	42%	
	% of total respondents	55%	7%	62%
MySpace		622	123	745
		21%	21%	
		18%	4%	21%
Browser toolbars		2269	482	2751
		77%	82%	
		64%	14%	78%
Text messaging		2037	436	2473
		69%	74%	
		58%	12%	70%
Mobile browsing		614	131	745
		21%	22%	
		17%	4%	21%
Web calling		1006	287	1293
		34%	49%	
		26%	8%	37%
Blackboard		1964	369	745
		67%	63%	
		56%	10%	66%

By academic status, undergraduates were much more receptive to Facebook library applications and slightly more receptive to library services in Blackboard, but were in general less receptive to potential and existing Library 2.0 services than graduate students (Table 7.1). These findings are somewhat consistent with observed social and mobile tool consumption patterns, which indicate that disruptive tools tend to be initially used by a niche audience and gradually adopted on a wider scale. My analysis indicates that students at Ohio University consume technology-based library services using a similar model, but that receptivity is more significantly motivated by higher age and academic status than it is by lower age, a higher technology adoption profile, or actual rates of social/mobile tool use and ownership. An inverse relationship emerges - graduate and older students are more likely to welcome the library utility of mobile and/or social tools they do not yet use or own, whereas undergraduates and younger students are less likely to see library utility of the tools they already use and own. In terms of graduate status, this inverse is directly related to relative levels of expressed information need and library website use. By virtue of higher information needs, graduate students either possess more highly developed personal learning environments, and/or are more likely to integrate new and innovative information tools into these environments.

On Interpreting Tables 7.2 and 7.3

Tables 7.2 and 7.3 were produced using multiple correlation analysis, a technique similar to that used to establish the correlation between academic and digital status in Chapter 4. Recall that the insight provided by correlation analysis does not explain how one variable affects another, only if and how often responses to one variable tend to reflect responses to another variable. As you view these tables remember that correlations measure the extent to which two variables are associated, and the direction of that association. A positively valued correlation indicates that as one variable increases the other variable increases (e.g. the higher academic status of a respondent, the higher their library website use). A negatively valued correlation indicates an inverse relationship, meaning that as one variable increases the other decreases (e.g. the lower the academic status of a respondent, the higher their rates of technology ownership). Positive correlations therefore describe effects with similar directions, whereas negative correlations describe effects with opposite directions. Positive correlations between variables are represented by a positive decimal, and negative correlations are represented by a negative decimal. While the relationship between lower age and lower library website use might appear to be negative because it describes downward trends, its correlation is actually positive (tau=.312). Similarly, the relationship between higher academic status and lower social software use is actually negative because it describes oppositional trends (tau= -.168).

In Chapter 4 I established a moderately strong positive correlation between academic and digital status (tau=.583), which indicated that graduate students were also likely to be digital immigrants. However, enough graduate students were classifiable as digital natives and vice versa to prevent the correlation from being perfect (in itself a statistical rarity). While all are still statistically significant, the strength of the correlations in tables 7.2 and 7.3 tends to be weaker than the academic status/digital status relationship. The significant correlations flagged in Tables 7.2 and 7.3 typically range from approximately .050 to .400, and can be thought to describe relationships that are less consistent or predictable. This may reflect the capricious nature of technology and library use among higher education students – patterns and predictability are challenging to establish.

Connecting Emerging Technologies

Whereas Table 7.1 establishes relative interest in emerging library technologies by academic status, Table 7.2 examines the relationships among student receptivity to different types of library technologies. This correlation matrix provides insight into the factors that may motivate student interest in different types of emerging library tools and applications such as Facebook, web browser customization, text messaging, and so forth. Because several variables in this matrix were not distributed on a normal bell-shaped probability curve, I selected Kendall's Tau-b as the most appropriate statistical method for correlation analysis (Morgan, 2004). Significance was calculated at the minimum level acceptable for the Social Sciences (.05). Correlations with a significance of .05 are flagged (*), as are those with a higher significance of .01(**). All of the nine significant correlations illustrated in this table are significant at the .01 level, and their effect sizes are small to medium according to the guidelines provided by Cohen (1988).

Table 7.2 Correlations Among Emerging Library Technology Receptivities

		Facebook	MySpace	Browser Toolbars	Text Messaging	Mobile Browsing	Web Calling
Facebook	Correlation Coefficient	1.000	.267(**)	.244(**)	.029	.132(**)	.173(**)
	Sig. (2-tailed)	.	.000	.000	.073	.000	.000
MySpace	Correlation Coefficient		1.000	.154(**)	.004	.249(**)	.204(**)
	Sig. (2-tailed)		.	.000	.852	.000	.000
Browser Toolbars	Correlation Coefficient			1.000	.031(*)	.154(**)	.151(**)
	Sig. (2-tailed)			.	.044	.000	.000
Text Messaging	Correlation Coefficient				1.000	.067(**)	.013
	Sig. (2-tailed)				.	.003	.396
Mobile Browsing	Correlation Coefficient					1.000	.270(**)
	Sig. (2-tailed)					.	.000
Web Calling	Correlation Coefficient						1.000
	Sig. (2-tailed)						.

**=Correlation is significant at the 0.01 level (2-tailed) *=Correlation is significant at the 0.05 level (2-tailed)

Student receptivity to Facebook library applications is positively correlated with receptivity to MySpace library applications (tau=.267), indicating that those well disposed towards one type of social software in a library context are likelier to be receptive to other social applications, even if their popularity is waning. Facebook library receptiveness among respondents is also correlated to interest in library browser toolbars (tau=.244), and modestly connected to mobile browsing and web calling library receptivity (tau=.132). Receptivity to mobile browsing and web calling services is the clearest correlation among all library technology receptivities (tau=.270). There is no observable correlation between texting and social software receptivity, or between texting and web calling receptivity.

Those who indicated receptivity to mobile library website use were the most likely to be receptive to all other forms of library service innovation. Interest in the mobile library web therefore emerges as the user characteristic most likely to indicate the confluence of high information need and early technology adoption status. The lack of negative correlations in Table 7.2 indicates the absence of inverse relationships among library technology receptivities. This suggests that in general terms, a predisposition toward one type of emerging library technology is associated with a similar predisposition to other technology types.

An Interplay of Factors

In order to address the full range of research questions outlined in Chapter 3 and to test conclusions reached in Chapters 4-6 by a different statistical method, Table 7.3 illustrates intercorrelations among a number of demographic, technological, and library use variables. This level of analysis goes beyond what is typically required of practical library environmental scanning, but it also illustrates connections between variables not identifiable using cross-tabulation. Because several variables were not distributed on a normal bell-shaped probability curve, I selected Kendall's Tau-b as the statistical method best suited to conduct correlational analysis (Morgan, 2004). Significance was calculated at a minimum of .05, acceptable for the Social Sciences. Correlations with a significance of .05 are flagged (*), as are correlations with a higher significance of .01(**). All but two of the forty-eight significant correlations illustrated in this table are significant at the .01 level. Similar to Table 7.2, effect sizes are small to medium according to Cohen's guidelines (1988).

Library Use

The most significant relationship between age/academic status and library behavior is in the area of student library website use. There is a positive correlation between higher age and increased frequency of library website visits and vice versa (tau=.312), indicating that the younger a respondent tended to be the less frequently they accessed the library website. The same trend is seen between higher academic status and increased library website use (tau=.331), indicating that older users and graduate students are similarly more inclined to be frequent library website users. A weak correlation is evident between age and in-person library visits (tau=.029), signaling that older users are only marginally more likely to use the physical library frequently respective to younger users. Similar relationships are evident between time spent online for pleasure and online time devoted to academics. Increased age is weakly associated with more time spent online per week (tau=.054), and more clearly related to a greater proportion of time spent online devoted to academic work (tau=.149).

Table 7.3 Correlations Among Age, Academic Status, and Library/Technology Use, Adoption, and Receptivity

		Age	Academic Status	Library Visits	Library Web Visits	Time Online	Academic Time Online	Technology Skill	Library/ Research Skill	Technology Adoption	Social Software Use	Technology Ownership	Library Tech Receptivity
Age	Correlation Coefficient	1.000	.583(**)	.029(*)	.312(**)	.054(**)	.149(**)	.031(*)	.229(**)	-.060(**)	-.157(**)	-.107(**)	.104(**)
	Sig. (2-tailed)	.	.000	.040	.000	.000	.000	.035	.000	.000	.000	.000	.000
Academic Status	Correlation Coefficient		1.000	-.007	.331(**)	.084(**)	.161(**)	.015	.203(**)	-.028	-.168(**)	-.119(**)	.097(**)
	Sig. (2-tailed)		.	.635	.000	.000	.000	.366	.000	.074	.000	.000	.000
Library Visits	Correlation Coefficient			1.000	.329(**)	-.012	.126(**)	.009	.104(**)	-.013	.018	-.086(**)	.072(**)
	Sig. (2-tailed)			.	.000	.393	.000	.551	.000	.377	.197	.000	.001
Library Web Visits	Correlation Coefficient				1.000	.061(**)	.178(**)	.074(**)	.296(**)	.003	-.067(**)	-.116(**)	.083(**)
	Sig. (2-tailed)				.	.000	.000	.000	.000	.846	.000	.000	.000
Time Online	Correlation Coefficient					1.000	-.079(**)	.130(**)	.046(**)	.154(**)	.092(**)	.070(**)	.034
	Sig. (2-tailed)					.	.000	.000	.002	.000	.000	.000	.102
Academic Time Online	Correlation Coefficient						1.000	.024	.095(**)	-.078(**)	-.151(**)	-.114(**)	.071(**)
	Sig. (2-tailed)						.	.100	.000	.000	.000	.000	.000
Technology Skill	Correlation Coefficient							1.000	.390(**)	.323(**)	.125(**)	.116(**)	.031
	Sig. (2-tailed)							.	.000	.000	.000	.000	.187
Library Skill	Correlation Coefficient								1.000	.096(**)	-.008	-.022	.072(**)
	Sig. (2-tailed)								.	.000	.595	.134	.001
Technology Adoption	Correlation Coefficient									1.000	.104(**)	.215(**)	.052(**)
	Sig. (2-tailed)									.	.000	.000	.018
Social Software Use	Correlation Coefficient										1.000	.129(**)	.052(**)
	Sig. (2-tailed)										.	.000	.018
Technology Ownership	Correlation Coefficient											1.000	.030
	Sig. (2-tailed)											.	.161
Library Tech Receptivity	Correlation Coefficient												1.000
	Sig. (2-tailed)												.

** = Correlation is significant at the 0.01 level (2-tailed) | * = Correlation is significant at the 0.05 level (2-tailed)

Technology Skill and Adoption

A slight but still significant correlation exists between age and self-perceptions of technology skill (tau=.031), indicating that higher age is only marginally associated with an increase in technology skill self-assessment. A clearer positive correlation exists between increased library website use and self-perception of high library and research skills (tau=.278). There are modest negative correlations between age and social software use (tau= -.157), and age and technology ownership levels (tau= -.107), indicating that social software use and technology ownership both tend to increase as age decreases. One of the strongest relationships demonstrated by the matrix is between self-perceptions of high library/research skills and high technology skills (tau=.390), which may be emblematic of the tendency of some respondents to inflate their own abilities. It may also reveal deeper connections between technology expertise and other types of information fluency, a topic that deserves further investigation. Increased time online is modestly connected to higher self-perception of technology skills (tau=.130) and only slightly to higher assessment of library skills (tau=.045). Age is slightly positively correlated with technology adoption status (tau= -.060). Self-perceptions of early technology adoption is positively associated with increased time spent online (tau=.154) and slightly higher self perception of library/research skills (tau=.096), but it is also negatively correlated with academic time spent online (tau= -.079). There is clear positive correlation between technology adoption status and higher self-perception of technology skills (tau=.380), indicating that perception of technology adoption increases as confidence in technology skills increases and vice versa.

Technology Use and Receptivity

Heavier social software use is modestly positively connected to higher self-perception of early technology adoption status (tau=.104), lower academic status (tau= -.168), and less frequent use of the library website (tau= -.067). Younger respondents were more likely to own a variety of communication and computing technologies than older respondents (tau= -.107), while a clearer connection between higher technology adoption and greater technology ownership is also evident (tau=.219). Higher age (tau=.104), academic status (tau=.098), increased frequency of library visits (tau=.072), increased frequency of library website visits (tau=.083) are all weakly but still significantly correlated with greater library technology receptivity. Library web usage is negatively correlated with technology ownership (tau= -.116), indicating a modest tendency towards less frequent library web use among respondents who own more technology.

Summary

According to Table 7.3 and findings outlined in Chapter 6, increased age and higher academic status are the clearest determining factors in overall library technology receptivity among Ohio University students. When this interest is unpacked, however, receptivity to specific tools simultaneously affirms and contradicts generational and demographic assumptions regarding higher education students and emerging technology use. Younger students are more receptive to library technologies via Facebook and Blackboard, findings that support their higher assumed interest in social and LMS-based technologies. A different pattern emerges for web and mobile communication services, however. Both web calling and text messaging library services are seen as more useful in a library context by graduate students, despite considerably greater undergraduate use of text messaging (relative to web calling, which is more used by graduate students).

The central point of my findings is this: although older students are relatively less likely to own and/or use multiple devices and social applications, they are clearly more receptive to the *idea* of using various technologies in a library context. Technology adoption status is not closely related to library technology receptivity, indicating that simply because a student self-identifies as an early technology adopter or owns and uses more technologies does not mean that they will be more inclined to adopt tools that enable research and information help.

Higher age, academic status, increased library website use, and more time spent online devoted to academics are closely correlated with most types of tech-based library receptivity. While all of these factors indicate increased age, they are also closely motivated by increased research and information need than any other variable. Graduate students are more inclined to conduct research and ask for information help via the library website, and are by extension more receptive to technology-based services that facilitate these processes. Undergraduates tend to be more frequent users of the library building for study or social purposes, activities that do not necessarily coincide with specific, library-related information needs.

Although increased library use is somewhat correlated with emerging technology receptivity, age has an inverse relationship to library website use and, by extension, most types of emerging technology receptivity. While younger users are more likely to own and use mobile and social technologies, older users are proportionally more receptive to library services offered via these and other innovative platforms with the exception of Facebook and Blackboard library applications, and then only slightly. As was shown by Table 6.4, respondents born before 1981 were twice as likely to express definite or potential interest in library technologies than those born after 1981.

Table 7.3 indicates that in terms of research need, intensity of library website use is chief among the factors that indicate receptivity to *visible* library technologies, or the category of library technology defined by the Scope Note in my Introduction. Visible technologies require intentional adoption and/or establishment of contact, while increased library website use indicates a greater dependence on research and information access tools. Beyond the simple predictor of academic status and social and mobile library service interest, the character and extent of library use is central to the motivation of these early library adopters, who are more likely to encounter new technologies via the library web than users with lower research and information needs. This point is further illustrated by the library technology receptivity of different academic majors. Respondents from tech-heavy disciplines such as engineering and other sciences may be the earliest adopters of emerging tools, but unless they are heavy library website users, their increased receptivity to library technologies is average. In short, those that rely most heavily on the library are the most inclined to use tech-based services, regardless of whether they use social and mobile tools proportionally heavily outside of the library.

Early Library Technology Adopters

My findings reveal a class of early *library* technology adopters among respondents, typically older and/or graduate students with high research/information needs, who do not necessarily mirror early technology adopters in wider society. By virtue of their research habits, these established and frequent library users are already well aware of many library services and are willing to integrate new tools into their already highly customized personal learning environments. These users view emerging tools as another aspect of research facilitation, and are more connected to academic endeavor than the merits of the technologies themselves.

I argue that these users also demonstrate what can be described as a *library predisposition*, or a tendency built on awareness to view library services in general as useful, regardless of delivery platform. Akin to a feeling of ownership and likely facilitated by a sense of familiarity and value, these high-use individuals are motivated by information need to perceive the necessity of libraries themselves, and by extension believe that library-provided technology tools may improve their overall academic experience. In essence, these users believe that *all* things library-related are good things. My research suggests that for these library-predisposed individuals, the existence of innovative library services may actually motivate their adoption of new technology platforms. These users, most often graduate students and older undergraduates, are the foundation of much of the library long tail, and likely already comprise of the user base of many pilot Library 2.0 programs.

Younger respondents are in general less aware of library services, and by extension less likely to demonstrate this predisposition (and by further extension likely to demonstrate a library disinclination). Analysis of undergraduate responses reveals that library awareness is a critical motivator not only in their adoption of emerging library technologies, but of their prospective library use overall. Consistent with a number of recent studies, low respondent familiarity of library service options communicates an incomplete understanding of the role and function of a typical academic library (Foster & Gibbons, 2007, OCLC, 2005).

Rather than being indifferent to their own lack of library awareness, analysis of open-ended comments reveals that students were either pleasantly surprised or slightly offended to realize how little they knew about library services. Undergraduates expressed a strong unsolicited desire to be better informed about library services - *even when they exhibited extremely low current levels of library and library website use* - and consistently encouraged the Libraries to more effectively market our resources. Many suggested strategies for how we could achieve this, such as visiting dorms and classes, flyering campus, and making announcements via Blackboard. That the OU Libraries already employ all of these methods starkly indicates the limitations of their reach, and suggests that even an extraordinarily service-oriented institution must continue to develop the ability to market itself.

Undergraduates and younger respondents were far more likely to indicate *potential* receptivity to library technologies, signifying that they are likely to believe that their information needs will change or become more demanding as they progress through their degree programs. Students expressed a consistent desire for greater awareness of all of their "library options," in order to facilitate the eventual use of resources on an as-needed basis. In this sense, the survey project itself unexpectedly became a powerful outreach tool, broadening both the library and technology awareness of thousands of OU students.

Findings suggest that while they may not engender immediate and widespread adoption, surveys and more direct marketing and education efforts will stimulate greater diffusion of awareness of library services throughout the student population as a whole, and among undergraduates in particular. I posit that this in turn will translate to increased use of traditional and technology-based services and spaces, potentially leading to a more prevalent library predisposition among undergraduates on a given campus. Brian Mathew's recent book, *Marketing Today's Academic Library*, contains a number of outreach and promotion strategies that may aid in promoting greater library understanding among all users.

Implications for Technology Service Development

While these findings are specific to Ohio University, they carry implications that can inform practical service development at other institutions. Those evaluating specific emerging tools for their ability to provide information services should consider the following factors:

1) *Social viability*. *Is the popularity of the tool or application in question rising or falling?* Once promising social tools that have been forcibly obfuscated by competition such as MySpace are far less likely to be viewed as useful in terms of student library experience. Student receptivity to library applications in MySpace vs. Facebook starkly demonstrates this effect. A library search/Ask a Librarian application in either of these social networks would theoretically perform the same functions, but student reaction to each was markedly different. The declining popularity of MySpace and its overwhelmingly negative characterization by students tempered their perception of its usefulness in a library context.

The more positive response to Facebook library applications illustrates the opposite side of this principle. That is, while student interest in Facebook applications was evenly split, because of its market primacy the tool was much more likely to be characterized as having legitimate academic applicability. Tellingly, opinion was divided not on the quality or popularity of Facebook itself, but on the appropriateness of its colonization by academic interests. In other words, students are more likely to evaluate whether a library treehouse is creepy or inviting if it is actually relevant to them.

Nascent platforms with a currently small but promising user base such as Twitter fall into another category altogether, and it is important to distinguish between emerging, established, and retreating tools.

Implication: Libraries developing services in potentially obsolescent social technologies (i.e. Second Life) should prepare for their potential decline or displacement by a competing tool or service. These technologies may still be useful in a *transparent* library context, and should therefore not be summarily dismissed. By virtue of their competitive nature, brand preference and competition among social tools in particular should factor into their evaluation in a library context.

2) *Technology disruption*. *To what extent has the technology been socially adopted, and how does this affect its viability as a library service?* Overall student receptivity to emerging library tools seems to increase in proportion to the extent of non-library adoption by the population at large. In the case of texting vs. web calling services, more students are receptive to text messaging, a technology that been available and commonly used for some time. IM reference services were not included in this survey because of their long-term success by the Ohio University Libraries, but they would likely be the most accepted form of patron-initiated contact of all methods investigated by this report. Longitudinal analysis of patron receptivity to various disruptive technologies is liable to demonstrate that non-obsolescent niche markets expand predictably over time. Similar to IM reference, as web calling and other tools such as Twitter become more prevalent a greater proportion of students will see their library-related communication potential. While it is reasonable to assume that web calling, text messaging, and mobile browsing will become increasingly applicable and desired within a library context, their present utility can still be described in terms of niche markets.

Implication: The current awareness and use of specific technologies will have a considerable effect on the corresponding audience size in library settings. A calculated assessment of future adoption potential should be made.

3) *Long-tail limitations.* *Early library technology adopters comprise small but enthusiastic niche markets for a variety of emerging services.* Libraries should understand the relatively small size of early library technology adopter populations and expect modest initial usage of "long tail" pilot programs. However, experimentation with web calling library services at Ohio University indicates that expectations of "successful" usage levels must be carefully considered for Library 2.0 services, and should be piloted experimentally and evaluated for their performance (Booth, 2008).

Due to the slow pace of technology disruption it is impossible for the relative success of IM reference to be duplicated by every new tech-based service. If seamless, user-focused technology integration succeeds on a number of levels, patron-initiated communication is likely to continue to become more distributed across multiple contact points, which may give the *appearance* of declining overall statistics as information needs actually become more efficiently addressed.

Implication: While a niche technology service may be highly appreciated by a small subset of users, this may not provide an acceptable rate of return on the staff time and other resources required to support it. The evaluation criteria of any pilot project should consider unacceptable levels of use.

4) *Convenience of integration. How seamlessly does the library technology in question integrate into the personal or academic learning environments of different students (social network, web browser, or learning management system)?* This factor confirms John Blyberg's idea of "seamlessness" and 2.0 service viability. If a library tool is a natural "fit" with a student's current technology and library profile, it is more readily identifiable as a helpful service by users of all demographics. Although Blackboard library options were not surveyed in precisely the same manner as the emerging or social tools included in Figure 7.1, library LMS integration nonetheless rivaled browser toolbars and Facebook applications as the most desired technology development option. Strong student interest in all of these platforms suggests the promise of library widgets and other applications that conveniently integrate into personally configured learning environments, or the academic side of a student's "personal web".

In the case of each interfaces, students perceive a high convenience factor in searching for library resources and/or receiving direct assistance from a librarian via tools that dovetail with their existing social, mobile, and academic access habits – for example, one user expressed interest in Facebook library options because "it would be an easier transition from my social online activities to actually doing homework." Verbatim responses also indicate that students are receptive to library technologies that allow them to leverage their own expertise in social and customizable technology tools. For many students, library interfaces are "too difficult," whereas social and personal search environments provide more comfortable and comprehensible avenues to conduct discover information.

Implication: Libraries should consider integrating emerging library services into preferred student search and discovery methods, because students are more likely to perceive these as a natural and desired fit with established information tools.

5) *Library awareness and information need. Higher library use results in greater receptivity to library technology innovation.* This may seem like an obvious connection, but when examined it carries significant implications for many new library services in terms of actual usage. A number of common assumptions concerning technology disruption and user demographics in higher education do not bear out in a library context, as demonstrated by greater digital immigrant and graduate student use

of and receptivity to all but Facebook and Blackboard library services. This phenomenon is illustrative of the ways in which degrees of information need influence library perceptions. Heavier library users, typically graduate students, older students, and advanced undergraduates, are more receptive to library services in general than infrequent library users, regardless of their technological profile. Undergraduates are far more likely to indicate potential rather than definite interest in emerging services, indicating that if they were to establish a stronger library profile they would be likely to see definite utility in various library technologies.

Because undergraduates vastly outnumber graduate students at typical research universities, the Pareto Principle or "80/20 rule" in library technology receptivity translates to a scenario wherein, on average, a fifth of the student library user base demonstrates high library use and high receptivity to emerging library services (graduate students), three-fifths of student users demonstrate average library use and some degree of receptivity to various emerging technology services (medium and high-use undergraduates), and the remaining fifth of students reflect inconsistent library use and low interest in emerging technology services (low-use undergraduates) (Lidwell, Holden, & Butler, 2003).

Implication: Libraries should anticipate that the most enthusiastic users of emerging technology library services will represent a small minority of the overall patron population, but that marketing and outreach efforts can still extend the reach of the library long tail.

Spreading Thin or Building Up?

In the absence of aggressive marketing and user education, the adoption of even mildly successful Library 2.0 tools may disperse established library users across a variety of access and information contact points, creating apparent rather than actual declines in library use. It takes a considerable amount of time for new markets to develop, and emerging tools may require ongoing revision before a suitable service model is located. With digital access and overall library contact points on the rise, users may find themselves better served remotely and/or less in need of direct communication via emerging or traditional methods.

The speed at which libraries and research needs are changing means that demand for emerging public services may not increase even when the user community expands proportionally. John Blyberg has written that "we're more likely to [fail] if we're arbitrarily introducing technology that isn't properly integrated into our overarching information framework... when we use technology, it should be transparent, intuitive, and a natural extension of the patron experience" (2008). Without adjusting the way we perceive a library's impact beyond traditional reference, web, and circulation statistics, an unintended result of Library 2.0 may be our incorrect inference that libraries are becoming less relevant when in reality they are simply becoming better at seamlessness.

Chapter 8: Conclusion

In the early years of the new millennium, many believed that information technology would create a hyperconnected youth culture with digital aptitudes far exceeding those of its predecessors. Authors such as Siva Vandayiathan and Henry Jenkins have since challenged this notion, arguing that sweeping generational divides obscure the social and ideological complexities of technology adoption and access. Their alternate perspectives confront the reality of disparate access and focuses on technology as a tool of adaptation, individual expression, and community building. As an indication of this shifting analytical focus, in a recent article Prensky rejects his own digital native/immigrant dichotomy, arguing that "when all have grown up in the era of digital technology, the distinction between digital natives and digital immigrants will become less relevant (2009, para. 1). Instead, he argues that a "digital humanity" will emerge that increasingly relies on *digital wisdom* to work and communicate, and that seeks to eradicate "digital dumbness," irresponsible or uninformed technology use such as plagiarism or cyberbullying. Digital wisdom "transcends the generational divide defined by the immigrant/native distinction" (para. 9), and reflects many of the traits librarians associate with the information literate individual.

As students progress through their academic experience, their understanding of how to construct a productive academic environment is shaped by need and experience. The idea of *digital residents* and *visitors* is a dichotomy more effective in describing this phenomenon: digital residents "[live] a percentage of their lives online," whereas digital visitors "[use] the web as a tool in an organized manner whenever the need arises" (White, 2008, paras. 2 & 3). The OU scan concludes that student receptivity to library technology innovation is more than a simple matter of generational affiliation. A student's personal *learning* web is a dynamic expression of their academic needs, social networking preferences, demographic characteristics, and awareness of the options that are available to them. Increasingly, information literacy will entail not only skills in discovery and analysis, but also the ability to achieve a desired level of personal technological customization in academic, work, social, and creative life. Toward this end, college and university libraries have much to contribute through education, outreach, research, and development.

The JISC/CIBER report, *Information Behaviour of the Research of the Future,* asserts that "in a real sense, we are all the Google generation now: the demographics of internet and media consumption are eroding... presumed generational difference[s]" (p. 21). In higher education, students use technology to fashion their learning environments in ways that contradict numerous age-based assumptions. My research at Ohio University points to a trait that is likely widely generalizable: while younger students tend to own and use more mobile and social tools, they have not necessarily reached the stage in their academic development that allows them to see their value in a research context. In a related sense, they do not exhibit the library predisposition demonstrated by older students, or the tendency to view our tools and services as inherently beneficial regardless of personal relevance.

In general, library technology receptivity was strongest among the oldest respondents regardless of academic standing. Paradoxically, these were also the least technology-engaged of all respondents. Does this point to a diminishing personal sense of library value among incoming cohorts of college students, or to a lack of current research needs and/or library awareness? Does this awareness gradually develop as academic needs become more acute? Are older students simply expressing their desire to become more conversant with emerging technologies, and consequently demonstrating a heightened sense of their promise in a research context? Would a greater research focus on library-as-place in this study have revealed a different library value system among younger students, one oriented more towards community endeavor and the overall library experience? My sense is that to some extent, all of the above are true. Despite their tendency to be less receptive to library technologies per se, open-ended commentary indicates that younger respondents were overwhelmingly receptive to confronting their own lack of library awareness. The shifting technology and literacy landscape sharpens our responsibility to encourage this awareness among all users, and to ensure that it is validated by libraries that enable positive and customizable digital and physical learning experiences.

Recommendations for Successful Library Technology Development

Our strength as service providers and our experience modifying social technologies positions academic librarians to facilitate and encourage this learning customization as an aspect of information and technology literacy. We can, however, only do so with more systematic insight into the social and organizational cultures that shape local needs. In order to create effective library technologies it is imperative that librarians better understand the communities we serve in order to inform an ongoing cycle of innovation. Active experimentation must be involved in this process, which requires the acceptance of risk, and organizational cultures that enable iterative approaches to service development. Wider adoption of a prototyping mentality, one that encourages "trying things out in the digital space, monitoring the reaction and adjusting accordingly" can help academic libraries meet the complex challenge of emerging technology development (JISC & CIBER, 2008, p. 31).

The modern academic library can develop a range of personalizable, practical tools adaptable to diverse student learning environments, but will only succeed if it does so based on insight and direct user feedback. Library 2.0's prescriptive utopianism has given way to an emphasis on technology as a means rather than an end. Social, mobile, and dynamic tools can be as capricious as they are beneficial, and it is not advisable to assume that the range of products commonly described as '2.0' are innately needed, anticipated, supportable, or effective. Many librarians are actively searching for strategies to identify technologies that are effective based not on their own merits, but on the realities of immediate user needs. Creating local cultures of assessment is a crucial part of this strategy, and should become pivotal to the process of fashioning adaptable, culturally attuned institutions. The OU environmental scan is an example of the cycle of research and response that can inform local decisions on an ongoing basis.

Lakos and Phipps write that "in the current external environment, libraries are challenged to be nimble, innovative, responsive, proactive and, most of all, able to demonstrate their value" (2004, p. 346). For a time, it seemed that emerging social and mobile technology technologies provided solutions to many, if not all, of these challenges. Revelations of the limited generalizability of Library 2.0 should not diminish the promise of new technologies to address problems and enhance the library experience. Much of the early criticism of "twopointopianism" hinged on the need for greater reflectiveness during the technology development process. Instead of mimicking the successes of peer institutions, academic librarians must sharpen their understanding of the cultures in which they operate in order to perceive where and when dynamic and social technologies are needed, wanted, and sustainable. The contextual unpredictability of these tools should simply motivate better planning grounded in the local version of reality. Innovation should become less viral, and should instead be more critical, flexible, purpose-driven, and practically integrated into the overall mission of the academic library.

I argue that that a number of conditions must be met in order to facilitate successful local climates of library innovation:

1) *research-based insight into local library, information, and technology cultures*
2) *knowledge of the universal characteristics of successful library technologies that can be applied in any context*
3) *understanding of local organizational structures/processes and their likely effect on technology planning and collaboration*
4) *active pursuit of working cultures that encourage prototyping, piloting, and experimentation*
5) *systematic planning for the implementation and assessment of emerging technology projects*
6) *a nuanced approach to library evaluation that takes into account the "long tail" effect of niche library services on overall usage statistics*
7) *a commitment to creative user outreach and education to raise the library profile*
8) *transparent internal and external communication during the assessment, development and evaluation process*

Lakos posits that library assessment cultures are "connected to the notion of systemic organizational change" (2007, p. 432). These conditions cannot be systematically achieved unless they are also supported, and library leaders should pay more than lip service to assessment, experimentation, and changing user expectations. It is critical to recognize the complementary roles that outreach and evaluation play in library effectiveness, and our collective ability to both internalize and externalize in a way that recognizes must be supported and encouraged throughout our organizations. Creating outwardly focused, reflective libraries that are adaptable to external change is an ongoing and surmountable challenge, and one that must be pursued in full recognition of the unique needs, characteristics, and library cultures that comprise each institution of higher learning. The experience of Ohio University clearly shows that in a supportive environment, homegrown cultures of assessment can be put to creative and multifaceted use.

My research indicates that the more clearly a student perceives the modern academic library, the more they are inclined to view its services as worthwhile. The same can be said for all users. Library sites and facilities are typically opaque enough to prevent understanding of our full range of utility, and assuming even a nominal degree of library awareness is unwise. The JISC/CIBER report urges libraries to "address the need for greater simplicity" in technology development as well as in the way we shape our physical buildings and collections, making them more accessible and intuitive based on local feedback (p. 30). It is equally important to address the need for greater awareness among both librarians and patrons. Local research offers critical insight into to the changing academic, human, and institutional cultures that influence library organizations, factors that can help us tailor our response to different user populations and encourage new library value systems.

The fundamental individuality of user, campus, and library cultures challenges the prescriptive approach to emerging library technology development advocated in the early days of Library 2.0. The relationships people form with our institutions vary based not only needs and demographic characteristics that may or may not be reflected in new technology projects, but also on the physical and digital conditions, quirks, and accumulated service history of the libraries they encounter – the personality or *gestalt* of a given library system. Ultimately, academic libraries are responsible for shaping our own gestalt, which I believe will increasingly come to form the foundation of the modern patron/library relationship.

If, as some argue, the intrinsic value of libraries is diminishing within academia and society as a whole, it then becomes our challenge to make this value more extrinsically evident. In other words, academic library users must not only come to understand how our institutions are changing, but should also be able to clearly perceive and define what makes libraries *personally* valuable on multiple levels. To facilitate this library predisposition among campuses and user communities, it is our responsibility to make our organizations more transparent, customizable, and consistent. To achieve this requires a renewed commitment to reflective assessment, ongoing professional development, organizational continuity, technological innovation, and aggressive user education.

References

Browser statistics. (2008). Retrieved July 13, 2008 from http://www.w3schools.com/

The cult of twopointopia. (2007, August 27). Message posted to
http://annoyedlibrarian.blogspot.com.

Blyberg, J. (2008, January 17). Library 2.0 debased. Message posted to http://www.blyberg.net/

Booth, C. (2008). Developing Skype-based reference services. *Internet Reference Services Quarterly, 13*(2/3), 147-165. Retrieved December 1, 2008, from Library, Information Science & Technology Abstracts database.

Booth, C. & Guder, C. (2009). If you build it, will they care? Tracking student receptivity to emerging library technologies. In D. Miller, Ed., *Pushing the edge: Explore, extend, engage. Proceedings, ACRL 14th National Conference.* Chicago: American Library Association.

Burgleman, J.C., Osimo, D., Pascu, C., Turlea, G., & Ulbrich, M. (2007). The potential disruptive impact of Internet 2 based technologies. *First Monday 12*(3). Retrieved August 10, 2008 from http://www.firstmonday.org/issues/issue12_3/pascu/

Caruso, J., Katz, R., Salaway, G., Kvavik, R., & Nelson, M. (2006). The ECAR study of undergraduate students and information technology. Retrieved July 3, 2008, from http://connect.educause.edu/ecar/

Caruso, J., & Salaway, G. (2007). The ECAR study of undergraduate students and information technology: Key findings. Retrieved July 3, 2008, from http://connect.educause.edu/ecar/

Cohen, J. (1988). *Statistical power and analysis for the behavioral sciences* (2nd ed.). Hillsdale, NJ: Lawrence Erlbaum Associates.

Chapman, S., Creech, M., Hollar, S., & Varnum, K. (2007). Main library gateway library web survey: Results and preliminary analysis. Unpublished study. Retrieved July 15, 2008, from http://www.lib.umich.edu/usability/projects/LibGateway.html

Council for Library and Information Resources. (2005). *Library as place: Rethinking roles, rethinking space.* Retrieved January 22, 2009, from http://www.clir.org.

Deiss, K., & Petrowski, M. (2009). ACRL 2009 strategic thinking guide for academic librarians in the new economy. Retrieved March 25, 2009 from http://www.ala.org/ala/mgrps/divs/acrl/issues/future/acrlguide09.pdf

DeRosa, C., Cantrell, J., Hawk, J., & Wilson, A. (2006). College students' perceptions of libraries and information resources: A report to the OCLC membership. Accessed June 20, 2008, from http://www.oclc.org/reports/perceptionscollege.htm

Drabinski, E. (2008, June 30). Letting ourselves fail. Message posted to http://librarypraxis.wordpress.com

Economist Intelligence Unit. (2008, October). *The future of higher education: How technology will shape learning.* Retrieved November 26, 2008, from Economist Intelligence Unit database.

Farkas, M. (2008, January 24). The essence of library 2.0? Message posted to http://www.meredith.wolfwater.com

Fister, B. (2008, May 17). Creepy treehouse. Message posted to http://acrlog.org/

Fitzpatrick, E., Moore, A., & Lang, B. (2008). Reference librarians at the reference desk in the learning commons: A mixed methods evaluation. *Journal of Academic Librarianship 34*(3) 231-238.

Foster, N. & Gibbons, S. (2007). *Studying students: The undergraduate research project at the University of Rochester.* Chicago: Association of Research Libraries. Accessed July 10, 2008, from http://docushare.lib.rochester.edu/docushare/dsweb/View/Collection-4436

Griffis, P., Costello, K., Del Bosque, D., Lampert, C., & Stowers, E. (2007). Discovering places to serve patrons in the long tail. In L. Cohen, Ed., *Library 2.0 initiatives in academic libraries*, (pp. 1-15). Chicago: Association of College and Research Libraries.

Horrigan, J. (2007). Typology of information and communication technology users. Retrieved July 3, 2008, from http://www.pewinternet.org/PPF/r/213/report_display.asp

Howe, N., & Strauss, W. (2000). *Millennials rising: The next greatest generation.* New York: Vintage Books.

Ito, M., Horst, H., Bittanti, M., boyd, d., Herr-Stephensen, B., Lange, P., Pascoe, C., & Robinson, R. (2009). *Living and learning with new media: Summary of findings from the digital youth project.* MacArthur Foundation Report on Digital Media and Learning. Retrieved January 23, 2009, from http://www.macfond.org.

Jenkins, H. (2007, December 5). Reconsidering digital immigrants... Message posted to http://www.henryjenkins.org/

Jenkins, H., Clinton, K., Purushotma, R., Robison, A., & Weigel, M. (2006). *Confronting the challenges of participatory culture: Media education for the 21st century.* MacArthur Foundation Occasional Paper. Retrieved July 15, 2008, from http://digitallearning.macfound.org/atf/cf/%7BE45C7E0-A3E0-4B89-AC9C-E807E1B0AE4E%7D/JENKINS_WHITE_PAPER.PDF

Johnson, L., Levine, A., and Smith, R. (2009). *2009 Horizon Report.* Austin, TX: The New Media Consortium, 2009. Retrieved January 23, 2009, from http://www.nmc.org/horizon/

Johnson, L., Levine, A., and Smith, R. (2008). *2008 Horizon Report.* Austin, TX: The New Media Consortium, 2008. Retrieved July 10, 2008, from http://www.nmc.org/horizon/

Johnson, L., Levine, A., and Smith, R. (2007). *2007 Horizon Report.* Austin, TX: The New Media Consortium, 2007. Retrieved July 10, 2008, from http://www.nmc.org/horizon/

Johnson, L., Levine, A., and Smith, R. (2006). *2006 Horizon Report.* Austin, TX: The New Media Consortium, 2006. Retrieved July 10, 2008, from http://www.nmc.org/horizon/

Johnson, L., Levine, A., & Smith, R. (2005). *2005 Horizon Report.* Austin, TX: The New Media Consortium, 2005. Retrieved July 10, 2008, from http://www.nmc.org/horizon/

Joint Information Systems Committee, & the Centre for Information Behaviour and the Evaluation of Research. 2008. Information behaviour of the researcher of the future. Retrieved July 20, 2008, from http://www.ucl.ac.uk/slais/research/ciber/downloads/

Jukes, I. (2007). Understanding the new digital landscape, kids, & the new "digital divide." Retrieved July 4, 2008, from http://web.mac.com/iajukes/thecommittedsardine/Home.html

Kelley, Brian. (2008). Library 2.0 and Information literacy: the tools. In P. Godwin and J. Parker (Eds.), *Information literacy meets Library 2.0*. London: Facet.

Lakos, A. (2007). Evidence-based library management: The library leadership challenge. *portal: Libraries and the Academy, 7*(4), pp. 431-450.

Lakos, A., & Phipps, S. (2004). Creating a culture of assessment: A catalyst for organizational change. *portal: Libraries and the Academy, 4*(3), pp. 345–361.

Lidwell, W., Holden, K., & Butler, J. (2003). *Universal principles of design*. Gloucester, Mass: Rockport.

Lenhart, A., Madden, M., McGill, A., & Smith, A. (2007). Teens and social media. Retrieved July 6, 2008, from http://www.pewinternet.org/PPF/r/230/report_display.asp

Lippincott, J. (2005). Net generation students and libraries. In D. G. Oblinger & J. L. Oblinger (Eds.), *Educating the net generation* (pp. 13.1-13.15). Boulder, CO: EDUCAUSE.

Lippincott, J. (2007). Student content creators: Convergence of literacies. *EDUCAUSE Review, 42*(6), 16-17.

Marcus, C., Covert-Vail, L. & Mandel, C. (2007). NYU 21st century library project: Designing a research library of the future for New York University. Retrieved October 8, 2008 from http://www.library.nyu.edu/about/KPLReport.pdf

Marcus, C., Ball, S., Delserone, L., Hribar, A., & Loftus, W. (2007). Understanding research behaviors, information resources, and service needs of scientists and graduate students: A study for the University of Minnesota Libraries. Retrieved November 1, 2008, from http://lib.umn.edu/about/scieval

McEuen, S. (2001). How fluent with information technology are our students? *EDUCAUSE Quarterly, 24*(4), 8-17.

Morgan, G. (2004). SPSS for introductory statistics: Use and interpretation. Mahwah, NJ: Lawrence Erlbaum.

Naylor, S., Stoffel, B., & Van Der Laan, S. (2008). Why isn't our chat reference used more?: Finding of focus group discussions with undergraduate students. *Reference & User Services Quarterly, 47*(4), 342-354. Retrieved December 1, 2008, from Library, Information Science & Technology Abstracts database.

Oblinger, D. G., & Oblinger, J. L., Eds. (2005). *Educating the net generation*. Boulder, CO: EDUCAUSE.

Ohio University fact book. (2007). Office of Institutional Research. Retrieved July 2, 2008, from http://www.ohiou.edu/instres/

Pin, W. (2007). Library 2.0: The new e-world order. *Library Connect Newsletter, 5*(4), 2. Retrieved July 7, 2008, from http://libraryconnect.elsevier.com/lcn/0504/lcn050402.html

Prensky, M. (2000). *Digital game-based learning*. New York: McGraw-Hill.

Prensky, M. (2001). Digital natives, digital immigrants: Part I. *On the Horizon, 9*(5), 1-6. Retrieved June 20, 2008, from http://www.marcprensky.com/writing/

Prensky, M. (2001). Digital natives, digital immigrants, part II: Do they really think differently? *On the Horizon, 9*(6) 15-24. Retrieved July 1, 2008, from http://www.marcprensky.com/writing/

Prensky, M. (2009.) H. sapiens digital: from digital immigrants to digital natives to digital wisdom. *Innovate: journal of online education, 5*(3). Retrieved February 2, 2009, from http://www.innovateonline.info/

Rogers, E. (2003). *Diffusion of innovations.* New York: Simon and Schuster.

Schmidt, P. (2008). 2 studies raise questions about research based on student surveys. *The Chronicle of Higher Education.* Retrieved November 7, 2008 from http://www.chronicle.com

Sclater, N. (2008). Web 2.0, personal learning environments, and the future of learning management systems. *Research Bulletin*, 13. EDUCAUSE Center for Applied Research. Retrieved July 7, 2008, from http://connect.educause.edu/Library/ECAR/ Web20PersonalLearningEnvi/46952

Servon, L. (2002). *Bridging the digital divide: Technology, community, and public policy.* Malden, MA: Blackwell.

Sheehan, K. (2008, January 16). Are librarians culturally self-aware? Message posted to http://loosecannonlibrarian.net/

Stein, J. (2008, April 9). Defining "creepy treehouse." Message posted to http://flexknowlogy.learningfield.org/

Stephens, M. (2008). Taming technolust: Ten steps for planning in a 2.0 world. *Reference and User Services Quarterly, 47*(4), 314-317.

Survey finds that only half of college students use e-books. (2008, June 28). *The Wired Campus Newsletter.* Retrieved July 4, 2008, from http://chronicle.com/wiredcampus/article/3115/survey-finds-that-half-of-college-students-dont-use-e-books

Sutton, L., & Bazirjian, R. (2009). Replication of the OCLC *Perceptions* study: The experience of two academic libraries. In D. Miller, Ed., *Pushing the edge: Explore, extend, engage. Proceedings, ACRL 14th National Conference.* Chicago: American Library Association.

Walker, J., & Jorn, L. (2007). Net generation students at the University of Minnesota, Twin Cities: Twin Cities student educational technology survey 2007. Retrieved October 16, 2008, from http://www.dmc.umn.edu/surveys/students/ssreport07.pdf

"Welcome to the Isthmus Project." (2008). Retrieved on 3 February, 2008, from http://isthmus.conted.ox.ac.uk/.

White, D. (2008, July 23). Not 'natives' & 'immigrants' but 'visitors' & 'residents'. Message posted to http://tallblog.conted.ox.ac.uk

Wilson, E. M. (in press). Academic library internet information provision model: Using toolbars and web 2.0 applications to augment subject reference. Proceedings of the 2009 American Society for Engineering Annual Conference & Exposition, Austin, TX. ASEE, Washington. Paper 471.

Vaidhyanathan, S. (2008). Generational myth: Not all young people are tech-savvy. *The Chronicle Review.* Retrieved November 10, 2008 from http://www.chronicle.com

Appendix A: Sample Survey

This Appendix is a modified and annotated version of the two online survey instruments administered in the Ohio University environmental scan - it is not an exact replica of the original instruments, and if used will therefore not produce results that can be benchmarked to our findings with the same degree of reliability. This sample document outlines a range of question types and subjects that may be useful in surveying local campus library and technology cultures. It is very comprehensive, and at times may appear redundant - instead of a ready-made survey, consider this a long-form template or bank of potential print or online questions that can be modified locally. Items are divided into sections using question headers, which you would not necessarily want to include in an actual survey. The questions in this instrument are geared toward a student respondent base, but could easily be modified to accommodate faculty and staff. Insights are provided in gray boxes throughout to help you consider the implications of certain design choices. If you adapt this sample instrument, keep a few things in mind:

1) Generally-worded questions and answer choices should be tailored to your specific context. Technology-related items should be careful carefully updated to reflect the most current tools, language, and trends.

2) In order to emphasize the importance of language in question neutrality, this revised instrument takes a relatively formal tone. The original instruments were somewhat more accessibly worded, using a more conversational tone at times.

3) There are many ways to inadvertently influence responses by the tone or orientation of a question. It is important to strive for neutrality and balance in both language and response options.

4) Shorter is typically better, and you should be mindful that the longer a survey takes to complete, the fewer responses you will receive. Select only necessary questions.

5) It is *imperative* to ask for review and commentary on a questionnaire after a first draft is created, both to spot errors and to gain different perspectives on the subjects, response choices, and question types you are using. Once a survey is released it cannot be changed in any significant way - an instrument should remain consistent for all participants, or its reliability will be undermined. In addition to peer or team feedback, you should recruit several individuals representative of the sample population to perform a trial run with your questionnaire. Afterwards, debrief them for their impressions of each item and its answer choices. Survey instruments are in general vastly improved by collaborative effort.

6) Likert Scale items (least to most, highest to lowest) typically offer five degrees of rating choices, whereas other types of scales can be more or less detailed. In order to present the broadest array of answer options, many scales included in this sample questionnaire are more detailed than those in the original surveys.

7) If used in their entirety, the array of items presented here would take considerable time to complete. The OU study was broken into two phases in order to allow us to be more comprehensive on each instrument. Brevity should be a goal of any survey, and each question should be carefully evaluated for its value in a local survey.

A) Demographic Information

1. How old are you?
- O 17-19
- O 20-22
- O 23-26
- O 27-30
- O 30

*Alternatively, use a drop-down menu to allow respondents to select their exact age. This may require more work to analyze than pre-segmented age

2. How did you find out about this survey?
- O Library website
- O Word of mouth
- O Email
- O Flyer
- O Instructor
- O Librarian
- O (Other _____)

*This type of item can inform how future surveys are promoted, and if a non-random sample is collected can help gauge influence or self-selection bias.

3. What best represents your major or concentration?
- O Business/Economics
- O Communications/Media Studies
- O Education
- O Engineering
- O Fine Arts/Design/Architecture
- O Humanities
- O Health Sciences
- O Physical Sciences
- O Computer Science
- O Social Sciences
- O Undecided
- O (Other _____)

*Options must be carefully worded to reflect departments/ majors at your institution, If an 'other' category is included that allows open-ended input, it is likely that a wide and problematic range of responses will be submitted.

4. Which of the following best describes you?
- O First-Year Undergrad
- O Second-Year Undergrad
- O Third-Year Undergrad
- O Fourth-Year Undergraduate
- O Fifth-year Undergraduate
- O Master's Student
- O PhD Student
- O Medical Student
- O Non-Degree
- O (Other _____)

*You can be general or specific with this type of item, depending on the depth of analysis you want to perform. It's easier to combine detailed response categories than to extract them after the fact. Depending on your research scope and purpose, you can also add a separate question to establish transfer student status.

5. What is your gender?
- O Male
- O Female
- O (I'd prefer not to say.)

*While it may seem like a given, you should consider the benefits of including a gender item carefully, as it may alienate respondents who have alternative gender identities or who prefer to keep this type of information private. Depending on what it adds to your analysis, you can add a neutral/anonymous item to the response choices, omit it entirely, or make gender an optional variable.

B) Library Use and Evaluation

1. On average, how often do you physically visit the library during the regular (quarter/semester)?

O Never
O Once a year
O Once per quarter/semester
O Monthly

O Weekly
O Several times per week
O Daily
O Several times a day

> ★The next two items pose an interesting problem, as student library use often fluctuates over the semester. Many only use libraries during finals week, or near an assignment due date. Provide a wide range of response options or specify "on average."

2. How often do you visit the library website during the regular (quarter/ semester)?

O Never
O Once a year
O Once per quarter/semester
O Monthly

O Weekly
O Several times per week
O Daily
O Several times a day

3. How many of the following options do you think the library currently offers? Check all that apply.

☐ Group study rooms
☐ Full-text articles online
☐ Talk with a librarian via IM or chat
☐ Research and library help classes
☐ Online tutorials
☐ Online article databases
☐ Research guides for different subject areas
☐ Talk with a librarian in person
☐ Scanners and multimedia software
☐ Cameras for checkout
☐ Request items from other libraries

☐ Full-text books online
☐ Call a librarian via Skype
☐ EBSCO article search
☐ Library news blog
☐ Online book/DVD renewals
☐ Get help writing a paper
☐ Movie viewing rooms
☐ Online library catalog
☐ DVDs for checkout
☐ Laptops for checkout
☐ [Etc., customize locally]

> ★This item can speak volumes about library awareness, and you may want to include only options currently available in your system to avoid giving false impressions. Customize answer choices to reflect local terminology, and consider placement directly before the general open-ended commentary item to gauge user reactions.

4. How often do you use the library website to do the following?

	Never	Once a year	Once per quarter/ semester	Monthly	Weekly	Several times a week	Daily	Several times a day
Ask a librarian for help or advice	O	O	O	O	O	O	O	O
Use research guides and tutorials	O	O	O	O	O	O	O	O
Find e-books	O	O	O	O	O	O	O	O
Search for articles	O	O	O	O	O	O	O	O
Search for books and journals	O	O	O	O	O	O	O	O
Access online reserves	O	O	O	O	O	O	O	O

5. When you are at the library, how often do you engage in the following?

	Never	Once a year	Once per quarter/ semester	Monthly	Weekly	Several times a week	Daily	Several times a day
Use library computers	O	O	O	O	O	O	O	O
Use your laptop	O	O	O	O	O	O	O	O
Do research for an assignment	O	O	O	O	O	O	O	O
Search for items in the catalog	O	O	O	O	O	O	O	O
Use the library website to find articles	O	O	O	O	O	O	O	O
Use the Cafe	O	O	O	O	O	O	O	O
Ask a librarian for help	O	O	O	O	O	O	O	O
Check out DVDs	O	O	O	O	O	O	O	O
Check out books/ journals	O	O	O	O	O	O	O	O
Use a group study room	O	O	O	O	O	O	O	O
Study alone	O	O	O	O	O	O	O	O
Study with friends	O	O	O	O	O	O	O	O
Pull an all-nighter	O	O	O	O	O	O	O	O
Socialize	O	O	O	O	O	O	O	O
Sleep	O	O	O	O	O	O	O	O
Listen to music	O	O	O	O	O	O	O	O

6. When you use a COMPUTER in the library [alt., a library computer], how often do you do the following?

	Never	Once a year	Once per quarter/ semester	Monthly	Weekly	Several times a week	Daily	Several times a day
Find books/articles	O	O	O	O	O	O	O	O
Use Blackboard	O	O	O	O	O	O	O	O
Check Facebook or MySpace	O	O	O	O	O	O	O	O
Use graphics software (Photoshop)	O	O	O	O	O	O	O	O
Use presentation software (PowerPoint)	O	O	O	O	O	O	O	O
Use word processing software (Word)	O	O	O	O	O	O	O	O
Use the library website	O	O	O	O	O	O	O	O
Check email	O	O	O	O	O	O	O	O
Use IM	O	O	O	O	O	O	O	O
Play video games	O	O	O	O	O	O	O	O
Watch online videos/DVDs	O	O	O	O	O	O	O	O

C) Information Use and Evaluation

1. How likely are you to use each of the following to START your research for an assignment?

	N/A – I don't use this resource.	Extremely unlikely	Unlikely	Somewhat likely	Likely	Extremely likely
Google	O	O	O	O	O	O
Wikipedia	O	O	O	O	O	O
Library catalog	O	O	O	O	O	O
Article database	O	O	O	O	O	O
Google Scholar	O	O	O	O	O	O
Ask friends/family	O	O	O	O	O	O
Ask my instructor	O	O	O	O	O	O
Ask a librarian	O	O	O	O	O	O

2. How easy is it to use the following to FIND resources for assignments?

	N/A – I don't use this resource.	Extremely difficult	Difficult	Neither hard nor easy	Easy	Extremely easy
Google	O	O	O	O	O	O
Wikipedia	O	O	O	O	O	O
Library catalog	O	O	O	O	O	O
Article database	O	O	O	O	O	O
Google Scholar	O	O	O	O	O	O
Ask friends/family	O	O	O	O	O	O
Ask my instructor	O	O	O	O	O	O
Ask a librarian	O	O	O	O	O	O

3. What is the overall QUALITY of information you find using the following?

	N/A – I don't use this resource.	Very low	Low	Fair	High	Very high
Google	O	O	O	O	O	O
Wikipedia	O	O	O	O	O	O
Library catalog	O	O	O	O	O	O
Article database	O	O	O	O	O	O
Google Scholar	O	O	O	O	O	O
Ask friends/family	O	O	O	O	O	O
Ask my instructor	O	O	O	O	O	O
Ask a librarian	O	O	O	O	O	O

D) Technology/Library Technology Use and Evaluation

1. How many hours per week do you spend online?
O Less than 5
O 6-10
O 11-20
O 21-30
O 31-40
O More than 40

> ★ Again, you could use a drop-down menu here to allow respondents to indicate an exact number. For this type of item, however, it is easier to estimate a general range and analyze responses using broader categories.

2. How much of this time is spent on school-related activities?
O 0%
O 1-25%
O 26-50%
O 51-75%
O 100%

> ★ We found that this was a very useful in determining relative levels of library/information need and research activity among respondents.

3. What kind of Internet connection do you have at home?
O Dial-up
O Broadband
O High-Speed wireless
O High-speed wired
O None
O Not sure

4. Which of the following best describes you?
O I usually avoid using new technologies.
O I generally take a while to use technologies.
O I use new technologies at the same time other people do.
O I tend to use new technologies somewhat before others do.
O I usually use new technologies before anyone else.

> ★This question can be a revealing and interesting way to analyze respondents, but it can be challenging to convey what is meant by "technology." You might want to specify "new technology tools and web applications," or list examples.

5. When you are researching, studying, or completing assignments, how often you do the following at the SAME TIME?

	Never	Infrequently	Sometimes	Usually	Always
Facebook, MySpace, etc.	O	O	O	O	O
Instant messaging	O	O	O	O	O
Online gaming	O	O	O	O	O
Text messaging	O	O	O	O	O
Mobile phone	O	O	O	O	O
Other (please specify): _____	O	O	O	O	O

6. How frequently do you do the following?

	Never	Once a year	Once per quarter/ semester	Monthly	Weekly	Several times a week	Daily	Several times a day
Text message	O	O	O	O	O	O	O	O
Instant message	O	O	O	O	O	O	O	O
Play online games	O	O	O	O	O	O	O	O
Play games on a console (PS3, XBOX 360, Wii, etc.)	O	O	O	O	O	O	O	O
Play handheld games (PSP, Nintendo DS, etc.)	O	O	O	O	O	O	O	O
Download music or videos	O	O	O	O	O	O	O	O
Listen to podcasts	O	O	O	O	O	O	O	O
Watch videos on YouTube	O	O	O	O	O	O	O	O
Use Skype or other web calling program	O	O	O	O	O	O	O	O
Use Facebook, MySpace, etc.	O	O	O	O	O	O	O	O
Post to a blog	O	O	O	O	O	O	O	O
Comment on a blog	O	O	O	O	O	O	O	O
Read a blog	O	O	O	O	O	O	O	O
Edit a Wikipedia article	O	O	O	O	O	O	O	O
Read Wikipedia articles	O	O	O	O	O	O	O	O
Receive search alerts	O	O	O	O	O	O	O	O

7. IF you own a mobile phone, how frequently do you use it to do the following? (If you don't own a mobile phone, skip ahead to item #x.)

	Never	Once a year	Once per quarter/ semester	Monthly	Weekly	Several times a week	Daily	Several times a day
Text message	O	O	O	O	O	O	O	O
Instant message	O	O	O	O	O	O	O	O
Use a search engine	O	O	O	O	O	O	O	O
Send email	O	O	O	O	O	O	O	O
Download music	O	O	O	O	O	O	O	O
Play games	O	O	O	O	O	O	O	O
Listen to podcasts	O	O	O	O	O	O	O	O
Watch videos	O	O	O	O	O	O	O	O
Read e-books	O	O	O	O	O	O	O	O
Check Facebook, etc.	O	O	O	O	O	O	O	O

8. IF you own a mobile phone, how likely would you be to use the following TEXT/SMS library services?

	I own a cell, but I don't text.	Extremely unlikely	Unlikely	Fairly likely	Likely	Extremely likely
Ask a librarian a question	O	O	O	O	O	O
Send a call number from the catalog	O	O	O	O	O	O
Receive renewal or overdue notices	O	O	O	O	O	O
Renew library materials	O	O	O	O	O	O

9. For each of the following gaming devices, select the phrase that best describes you.

	Don't own it, don't care.	Used to own it.	Own it.	Wish I owned it.
Nintendo Wii	O	O	O	O
Nintendo DS	O	O	O	O
Gameboy	O	O	O	O
XBOX	O	O	O	O
XBOX 360	O	O	O	O
Sony PS1	O	O	O	O
Sony PS2	O	O	O	O
Sony PS3	O	O	O	O
PSP	O	O	O	O
Oldschool Nintendo, Sega or Atari system	O	O	O	O

10. For each of these web tools and social sites, select the phrase that best describes you.

	Never heard of it.	Never use it.	Used to use it.	Using it less lately.	Using it more lately.	Use it all the time.
Facebook	O	O	O	O	O	O
MySpace	O	O	O	O	O	O
Friendster	O	O	O	O	O	O
Bebo	O	O	O	O	O	O
LinkedIn	O	O	O	O	O	O
Second Life	O	O	O	O	O	O
Delicious	O	O	O	O	O	O
Skype	O	O	O	O	O	O
Twitter	O	O	O	O	O	O
Zotero	O	O	O	O	O	O
Other: _____	O	O	O	O	O	O

11. Which of the following Google tools do you currently use? Check all that apply.

- ☐ Search
- ☐ Gmail
- ☐ Book search
- ☐ Documents
- ☐ Reader
- ☐ Labs
- ☐ Maps
- ☐ Calendar
- ☐ Groups
- ☐ Scholar
- ☐ Personalized home page (iGoogle)
- ☐ Search alerts
- ☐ News
- ☐ Video
- ☐ Image search
- ☐ Talk
- ☐ Other: _____

12. Which of the following do you own? Check all that apply.

- ☐ Laptop computer
- ☐ Desktop computer
- ☐ PDA
- ☐ Portable media player (iPod)
- ☐ Digital camera
- ☐ Digital video recorder
- ☐ [Etc., customize]

13. What web browser do you prefer?

- O Mozilla Firefox
- O Internet Explorer
- O Safari
- O Opera
- O Not sure
- O No preference
- O Other: _____

14. Do you customize your web browser with add-ons, extensions, and/or toolbars?

- O Yes
- O No
- O Not sure

15. If they were available, would you use library web browser extensions and search toolbars?

- O Yes
- O No
- O (Maybe)

Why or why not?

★ The following two items are alternate ways to gauge library receptivity to a number of tools and technologies. It is important to suggest potential uses of each technology in a library setting, so that respondents have a talk-based understanding of what the question is getting at. Asking why or why not provides invaluable feedback into how students use (library) technology in personal learning environments. Including "maybe" or "might use" is a difficult answer type to interpret, but it can help indicate a student's perception of potential use for the item in question.

16. How likely would you be to use the following library services in [your learning management system]?

	My classes don't use [the LMS]	Extremely unlikely	Unlikely	Fairly likely	Likely	Extremely likely
Ask a librarian chat	O	O	O	O	O	O
Article search box	O	O	O	O	O	O
Library/ research tutorials	O	O	O	O	O	O
Catalog search box	O	O	O	O	O	O

17. Which of the following have you used in your classes or coursework? Check all that apply.
- ☐ Blogs
- ☐ Wikis
- ☐ Podcasts
- ☐ Webcasts
- ☐ Online screencast tutorials
- ☐ Virtual worlds (Second Life, etc.)

18. Have you ever taken an online course or courses at [your institution]? Check all that apply.
- ☐ Yes, it was entirely online.
- ☐ Yes, but it met face-to-face as well.
- ☐ Neither

E) Open-Ended Library Evaluation

1. What do you MOST appreciate about [your campus library]?

> *This type of open-ended item can bring important personal insight to mostly closed-form surveys. It is important to offer respondents the chance to describe their own library experience, rather than pre-defining all answer categories. An alternative wording could be to ask about the library's 'best' aspects, etc.

2. What do you LEAST appreciate about [your campus library]?

> *Specifying your library by name will generate significantly different responses than asking for user impressions of libraries in general. General insights on library impressions can be interesting, but specific feedback on your institution gives the best practical insight.

3. Do you have any other comments or suggestions?

> *This type of item allows the respondent to speak to whatever might be on their mind, and is excellent for gathering unexpected insights and feedback as well as heartfelt praise or criticism. This item generally functions well towards the end of a survey, as other questions can inspire a comment or realization that arises from the educational effect of the survey instrument itself.

Appendix B: Sample Library/Technology Profile for 1st-Year Outreach Librarian

After a data set of survey responses is imported into SPSS, Excel, Access or other statistical/database program, it can be used for a number of purposes beyond creating a basic report of findings. This Appendix is an example of a sample custom user profile, created in an on-the-fly consultation with Sherri Saines, the Ohio University First-Year Outreach Librarian, using the technique described in Chapter 3. It illustrates the depth of practical insight that can be produced by segmenting survey results based on demographic variables such as major, age, and gender against more complex variables such as research skill self-assessment and library website use.

Areas of particular difference between first-year students and the rest of the population (Part 1) and between first-years and fourth-years (Part 2) are highlighted in gray. Analysis variables are identified in the title of each table, and at times both the count (number of respondents) and the percentage of responses are listed. Tables appear below in the standard output style produced by SPSS, which is highly customizable and exportable in a number of document formats such as Microsoft Word and PDF. At times, letters used to label and identify variables in SPSS are visible, such as q (quality), e (ease of use) and s (starting point for research).

Part 1 - Survey 1 Analysis

Frequency of library visits * first years Crosstabulation

			first years		Total
			first-year students	everyone else	
Frequency of library visits	Never	Count	24	117	141
		% within first years	2.7%	4.3%	3.9%
	Monthly	Count	232	670	902
		% within first years	25.7%	24.4%	24.7%
	Weekly	Count	335	835	1170
		% within first years	37.1%	30.4%	32.1%
	Several times a week	Count	255	871	1126
		% within first years	28.3%	31.7%	30.9%
	Daily	Count	56	253	309
		% within first years	6.2%	9.2%	8.5%
Total		Count	902	902	2746
		% within first years	100.0%	100.0%	100.0%

Frequency of library website visits * first years Crosstabulation

			first years		Total
			first-year students	everyone else	
Frequency of library website visits	Never	Count	299	320	619
		% within first years	33.1%	11.7%	17.0%
	Monthly	Count	257	703	960
		% within first years	28.5%	25.6%	26.3%
	Weekly	Count	228	762	990
		% within first years	25.3%	27.7%	27.1%
	Several times a week	Count	100	701	801
		% within first years	11.1%	25.5%	22.0%
	Daily	Count	18	260	278
		% within first years	2.0%	9.5%	7.6%
Total		Count	902	2746	3648
		% within first years	100.0%	100.0%	100.0%

Library Website Use *first years Crosstabulation

			first years		Total
			first-year students	everyone else	
library website use	Search for books and journals	Count	339	972	1311
		% within rfirst	37.6%	35.4%	
	Search for articles in a database	Count	646	1959	2605
		% within rfirst	71.6%	71.4%	
	Search for DVDs and music	Count	574	1668	2242
		% within rfirst	63.6%	60.8%	
	Use InfoTree to find articles and websites	Count	365	1154	1519
		% within rfirst	40.5%	42.0%	
	Use research guides and tutorials	Count	134	425	559
		% within rfirst	14.9%	15.5%	
	Ask a librarian for help or advice	Count	139	401	540
		% within rfirst	15.4%	14.6%	
Total		Count	902	2745	3647

Self-assessment of locating books and articles * first years Crosstabulation

		first years		Total
		first-year students	everyone else	
Self-assessment of locating books and articles	least skilled	4.1%	1.8%	2.4%
	somewhat skilled	12.6%	5.4%	7.2%
	moderately skilled	36.1%	25.0%	27.7%
	very skilled	37.0%	42.6%	41.2%
	most skilled	10.1%	25.2%	21.5%
Total		100.0%	100.0%	100.0%

Self-assessment of Blackboard skills * first years Crosstabulation

		first years		Total
		first-year students	everyone else	
Self-assessment of Blackboard skills	least skilled	.7%	1.0%	.9%
	somewhat skilled	1.6%	2.3%	2.1%
	moderately skilled	10.9%	7.4%	8.3%
	very skilled	38.9%	33.2%	34.6%
	most skilled	48.0%	56.1%	54.1%
Total		100.0%	100.0%	100.0%

Self-assessment of web design skills * first years Crosstabulation

		first years		Total
		first-year students	everyone else	
Self-assessment of web design skills	least skilled	37.8%	40.7%	40.0%
	somewhat skilled	28.7%	27.0%	27.4%
	moderately skilled	19.7%	17.8%	18.3%
	very skilled	10.3%	9.1%	9.4%
	most skilled	3.4%	5.5%	5.0%
Total		100.0%	100.0%	100.0%

Self-assessment of graphics software skills * first years Crosstabulation

		first years		Total
		first-year students	everyone else	
Self-assessment of graphics software skills	least skilled	17.2%	17.8%	17.7%
	somewhat skilled	25.9%	24.5%	24.9%
	moderately skilled	29.4%	29.6%	29.6%
	very skilled	19.6%	18.1%	18.4%
	most skilled	7.9%	10.0%	9.5%
Total		100.0%	100.0%	100.0%

Self-assessment of presentation software skills * first years Crosstabulation

		first years		Total
		first-year students	everyone else	
Self-assessment of presentation software skills	least skilled	2.0%	1.9%	1.9%
	somewhat skilled	7.2%	5.9%	6.2%
	moderately skilled	26.3%	21.4%	22.6%
	very skilled	40.0%	39.7%	39.7%
	most skilled	24.5%	31.2%	29.6%
Total		100.0%	100.0%	100.0%

Self-assessment of word processing skills * first years Crosstabulation

		first years		Total
		first-year students	everyone else	
Self-assessment of word processing skills	least skilled	.4%	.4%	.4%
	somewhat skilled	1.2%	1.0%	1.0%
	moderately skilled	9.2%	6.0%	6.8%
	very skilled	36.3%	32.2%	33.2%
	most skilled	52.9%	60.5%	58.6%
Total		100.0%	100.0%	100.0%

Self-assessment of library skills * first years Crosstabulation

		first years		Total
		first-year students	everyone else	
Self-assessment of library skills	least skilled	3.8%	1.8%	2.3%
	somewhat skilled	17.3%	9.3%	11.3%
	moderately skilled	39.0%	32.5%	34.1%
	very skilled	32.4%	40.3%	38.3%
	most skilled	7.5%	16.1%	14.0%
Total		100.0%	100.0%	100.0%

Self-assessment of computer troubleshooting abilities * first years Crosstabulation

		first years		Total
		first-year students	everyone else	
Self-assessment of computer troubleshooting abilities	least skilled	33.3%	34.3%	34.0%
	somewhat skilled	27.7%	22.8%	24.0%
	moderately skilled	22.0%	21.7%	21.7%
	very skilled	12.5%	14.2%	13.8%
	most skilled	4.5%	7.0%	6.4%
Total		100.0%	100.0%	100.0%

Use library computers * first years Crosstabulation

		first years		Total
		first-year students	everyone else	
Use library computers	never	6.7%	6.0%	6.2%
	monthly	27.7%	22.5%	23.6%
	weekly	27.7%	25.1%	25.7%
	several times a week	24.8%	27.8%	27.1%
	daily	13.1%	18.5%	17.4%
Total		100.0%	100.0%	100.0%

Do research for an assignment * first years Crosstabulation

		first years		Total
		first-year students	everyone else	
Do research for an assignment	never	10.6%	7.6%	8.2%
	monthly	48.4%	39.7%	41.6%
	weekly	26.4%	28.1%	27.7%
	several times a week	10.6%	18.0%	16.5%
	daily	4.1%	6.6%	6.1%
Total		100.0%	100.0%	100.0%

Search for items in ALICE * first years Crosstabulation

		first years		Total
		first-year students	everyone else	
Search for items in ALICE	never	14.7%	9.3%	10.4%
	monthly	44.9%	38.2%	39.6%
	weekly	25.8%	28.2%	27.7%
	several times a week	10.6%	18.0%	16.4%
	daily	4.1%	6.3%	5.8%
Total		100.0%	100.0%	100.0%

Use InfoTree to find articles and websites * first years Crosstabulation

		first years		Total
		first-year students	everyone else	
Use InfoTree to find articles and websites	never	26.8%	20.3%	21.7%
	monthly	42.9%	37.6%	38.7%
	weekly	19.1%	23.7%	22.7%
	several times a week	9.4%	13.5%	12.6%
	daily	1.8%	5.0%	4.3%
Total		100.0%	100.0%	100.0%

Buy something at Cafe Bibliotech * first years Crosstabulation

		first years		Total
		first-year students	everyone else	
Buy something at Cafe Bibliotech	never	48.1%	42.4%	43.6%
	monthly	28.2%	32.0%	31.2%
	weekly	15.0%	15.1%	15.1%
	several times a week	6.7%	8.2%	7.9%
	daily	2.1%	2.2%	2.2%
Total		100.0%	100.0%	100.0%

Ask a librarian for help or advice   * first years Crosstabulation

		first years		Total
		first-year students	everyone else	
Ask a librarian for help or advice	never	27.5%	27.6%	27.6%
	monthly	44.1%	51.4%	49.8%
	weekly	20.3%	15.5%	16.5%
	several times a week	6.7%	4.2%	4.7%
	daily	1.4%	1.3%	1.3%
Total		100.0%	100.0%	100.0%

Check out DVDs or music * first years Crosstabulation

		first years		Total
		first-year students	everyone else	
Check out DVDs or music	never	33.8%	37.6%	36.8%
	monthly	40.6%	36.6%	37.5%
	weekly	17.9%	16.5%	16.8%
	several times a week	6.2%	7.4%	7.1%
	daily	1.5%	2.0%	1.9%
Total		100.0%	100.0%	100.0%

Check out books * first years Crosstabulation

		first years		Total
		first-year students	everyone else	
Check out books	never	26.9%	21.4%	22.6%
	monthly	55.6%	48.1%	49.7%
	weekly	12.6%	19.7%	18.2%
	several times a week	3.8%	8.2%	7.3%
	daily	1.2%	2.6%	2.3%
Total		100.0%	100.0%	100.0%

Use a group study room * first years Crosstabulation

		first years		Total
		first-year students	everyone else	
Use a group study room	never	39.1%	38.2%	38.4%
	monthly	45.3%	41.3%	42.2%
	weekly	8.9%	11.6%	11.0%
	several times a week	5.6%	7.3%	6.9%
	daily	1.2%	1.7%	1.6%
Total		100.0%	100.0%	100.0%

Part 2 - Survey 2 Analysis

Academic Status

		Frequency	Percent	Valid Percent	Cumulative Percent
Valid	1st-year undergraduate	347	21.0	21.0	21.0
	2nd-year undergraduate	352	21.3	21.3	42.3
	3rd-year undergraduate	293	17.7	17.7	60.1
	4th-year undergraduate	241	14.6	14.6	74.7
	5th-year undergraduate	73	4.4	4.4	79.1
	master's student	192	11.6	11.6	90.7
	PhD student	101	6.1	6.1	96.9
	non-traditional or other	52	3.1	3.1	100.0
	Total	1651	100.0	100.0	

Use library computers * first-years vs. fourth-years Crosstabulation

		first-year students	fourth-year students	Total
Use library computers	never	6.7%	4.2%	5.7%
	monthly	27.7%	23.4%	25.9%
	weekly	27.7%	24.7%	26.5%
	several times a week	24.8%	28.0%	26.1%
	daily	13.1%	19.7%	15.8%
Total		100.0%	100.0%	100.0%

Do research for an assignment * first-years vs. fourth-years Crosstabulation

		first-year students	fourth-year students	Total
Do research for an assignment	never	10.6%	6.4%	8.8%
	monthly	48.4%	43.6%	46.4%
	weekly	26.4%	25.0%	25.8%
	several times a week	10.6%	20.3%	14.6%
	daily	4.1%	4.7%	4.3%
Total		100.0%	100.0%	100.0%

Search for items in ALICE * first-years vs. fourth-years Crosstabulation

		first-year students	fourth-year students	Total
Search for items in ALICE	never	14.7%	9.3%	12.5%
	monthly	44.9%	46.8%	45.7%
	weekly	25.8%	24.9%	25.4%
	several times a week	10.6%	16.0%	12.8%
	daily	4.1%	3.0%	3.6%
Total		100.0%	100.0%	100.0%

Use InfoTree to find articles and websites * first-years vs. fourth-years Crosstabulation

| | | first-years vs. fourth-years | | |
		first-year students	fourth-year students	Total
Use InfoTree to find articles and websites	never	26.8%	16.1%	22.4%
	monthly	42.9%	44.5%	43.6%
	weekly	19.1%	20.8%	19.8%
	several times a week	9.4%	14.8%	11.6%
	daily	1.8%	3.8%	2.6%
Total		100.0%	100.0%	100.0%

Buy something at Cafe Bibliotech * first-years vs. fourth-years Crosstabulation

| | | first-years vs. fourth-years | | |
		first-year students	fourth-year students	Total
Buy something at Cafe Bibliotech	never	48.1%	36.9%	43.5%
	monthly	28.2%	38.1%	32.2%
	weekly	15.0%	14.4%	14.7%
	several times a week	6.7%	9.3%	7.8%
	daily	2.1%	1.3%	1.7%
Total		100.0%	100.0%	100.0%

Ask a librarian for help or advice * first-years vs. fourth-years Crosstabulation

| | | first-years vs. fourth-years | | |
		first-year students	fourth-year students	Total
Ask a librarian for help or advice	never	27.5%	31.1%	29.0%
	monthly	44.1%	52.1%	47.3%
	weekly	20.3%	13.0%	17.3%
	several times a week	6.7%	3.4%	5.3%
	daily	1.4%	.4%	1.0%
Total		100.0%	100.0%	100.0%

Check out DVDs or music * first-years vs. fourth-years Crosstabulation

| | | first-years vs. fourth-years | | |
		first-year students	fourth-year students	Total
Check out DVDs or music	never	33.8%	43.3%	37.8%
	monthly	40.6%	37.5%	39.3%
	weekly	17.9%	14.2%	16.4%
	several times a week	6.2%	4.6%	5.5%
	daily	1.5%	.4%	1.0%
Total		100.0%	100.0%	100.0%

Check out books * first-years vs. fourth-years Crosstabulation

		first-years vs. fourth-years		Total
		first-year students	fourth-year students	
Check out books	never	26.9%	24.8%	26.0%
	monthly	55.6%	50.4%	53.4%
	weekly	12.6%	18.5%	15.0%
	several times a week	3.8%	5.5%	4.5%
	daily	1.2%	.8%	1.0%
Total		100.0%	100.0%	100.0%

Use a group study room * first-years vs. fourth-years Crosstabulation

		first-years vs. fourth-years		Total
		first-year students	fourth-year students	
Use a group study room	never	39.1%	30.8%	35.7%
	monthly	45.3%	48.5%	46.6%
	weekly	8.9%	10.1%	9.4%
	several times a week	5.6%	8.9%	7.0%
	daily	1.2%	1.7%	1.4%
Total		100.0%	100.0%	100.0%

Start research with Wikipedia * first-years vs. fourth-years Crosstabulation

		first-years vs. fourth-years		Total
		first-year students	fourth-year students	
sWikipedia	not likely	26.2%	28.1%	27.0%
	somewhat likely	22.8%	19.0%	21.2%
	likely	18.5%	20.8%	19.4%
	very likely	14.2%	15.6%	14.7%
	extremely likely	18.5%	16.5%	17.6%
Total		100.0%	100.0%	100.0%

Start research with Google * first-years vs. fourth-years Crosstabulation

		first-years vs. fourth-years		Total
		first-year students	fourth-year students	
sGoogle	not likely	3.2%	5.8%	4.3%
	somewhat likely	8.8%	5.8%	7.6%
	likely	16.7%	17.9%	17.2%
	very likely	24.3%	21.7%	23.2%
	extremely likely	47.1%	48.8%	47.8%
Total		100.0%	100.0%	100.0%

Start research with ALICE * first-years vs. fourth-years Crosstabulation

		first-years vs. fourth-years		Total
		first-year students	fourth-year students	
sALICE	not likely	13.3%	4.6%	9.7%
	somewhat likely	17.2%	25.7%	20.8%
	likely	29.9%	25.3%	28.0%
	very likely	28.7%	25.3%	27.3%
	extremely likely	10.9%	19.0%	14.3%
Total		100.0%	100.0%	100.0%

Start research with Academic Search Complete * first-years vs. fourth-years Crosstabulation

		first-years vs. fourth-years		Total
		first-year students	fourth-year students	
sAcademic Search Complete	not likely	25.0%	15.5%	21.1%
	somewhat likely	18.2%	16.4%	17.5%
	likely	23.4%	25.6%	24.3%
	very likely	21.1%	26.5%	23.3%
	extremely likely	12.3%	16.0%	13.9%
Total		100.0%	100.0%	100.0%

Start research with Library website * first-years vs. fourth-years Crosstabulation

		first-years vs. fourth-years		Total
		first-year students	fourth-year students	
sLibrary website	not likely	15.6%	8.1%	12.5%
	somewhat likely	18.9%	26.7%	22.1%
	likely	27.2%	29.2%	28.1%
	very likely	28.1%	17.8%	23.9%
	extremely likely	10.2%	18.2%	13.5%
Total		100.0%	100.0%	100.0%

Start research with OU Website * first-years vs. fourth-years Crosstabulation

		first-years vs. fourth-years		Total
		first-year students	fourth-year students	
sOU Website	not likely	30.7%	39.5%	34.4%
	somewhat likely	23.5%	30.0%	26.3%
	likely	22.3%	18.5%	20.7%
	very likely	17.9%	6.9%	13.2%
	extremely likely	5.6%	5.2%	5.4%
Total		100.0%	100.0%	100.0%

Start research with Google Scholar * first-years vs. fourth-years Crosstabulation

		first-years vs. fourth-years		
		first-year students	fourth-year students	Total
sGoogle Scholar	not likely	32.2%	32.2%	32.2%
	somewhat likely	19.1%	24.9%	21.5%
	likely	22.6%	20.5%	21.7%
	very likely	15.5%	10.7%	13.5%
	extremely likely	10.6%	11.7%	11.1%
Total		100.0%	100.0%	100.0%

Start research with EBSCO * first-years vs. fourth-years Crosstabulation

		first-years vs. fourth-years		
		first-year students	fourth-year students	Total
sEBSCO	not likely	26.5%	27.1%	26.8%
	somewhat likely	20.1%	15.9%	18.3%
	likely	21.4%	22.9%	22.0%
	very likely	18.4%	20.6%	19.3%
	extremely likely	13.6%	13.6%	13.6%
Total		100.0%	100.0%	100.0%

Start research with Article database or index * first-years vs. fourth-years Crosstabulation

		first-years vs. fourth-years		
		first-year students	fourth-year students	Total
sArticle database or index	not likely	24.0%	20.4%	22.5%
	somewhat likely	21.4%	22.6%	21.9%
	likely	28.9%	25.2%	27.3%
	very likely	15.6%	20.8%	17.8%
	extremely likely	10.1%	11.1%	10.5%
Total		100.0%	100.0%	100.0%

Ease of research Wikipedia * first-years vs. fourth-years Crosstabulation

		first-years vs. fourth-years		
		first-year students	fourth-year students	Total
eWikipedia	very difficult	9.1%	3.2%	6.7%
	difficult	6.6%	5.4%	6.1%
	average	11.7%	14.0%	12.6%
	easy	18.0%	17.6%	17.8%
	very easy	54.6%	59.9%	56.8%
Total		100.0%	100.0%	100.0%

Ease of research Google * first-years vs. fourth-years Crosstabulation

		first-years vs. fourth-years		Total
		first-year students	fourth-year students	
eGoogle	very difficult	8.1%	3.3%	6.2%
	difficult	5.5%	5.4%	5.5%
	average	12.5%	11.7%	12.2%
	easy	22.6%	28.5%	25.0%
	very easy	51.3%	51.0%	51.2%
Total		100.0%	100.0%	100.0%

Ease of research ALICE * first-years vs. fourth-years Crosstabulation

		first-years vs. fourth-years		Total
		first-year students	fourth-year students	
eALICE	very difficult	4.8%	2.1%	3.7%
	difficult	11.5%	12.0%	11.7%
	average	30.0%	36.5%	32.8%
	easy	32.6%	32.2%	32.4%
	very easy	21.1%	17.2%	19.4%
Total		100.0%	100.0%	100.0%

Ease of research Academic Search Complete * first-years vs. fourth-years Crosstabulation

		first-years vs. fourth-years		Total
		first-year students	fourth-year students	
eAcademic Search Complete	very difficult	4.6%	3.2%	4.0%
	difficult	13.8%	13.2%	13.6%
	average	38.7%	38.1%	38.4%
	easy	25.3%	31.2%	27.8%
	very easy	17.6%	14.3%	16.2%
Total		100.0%	100.0%	100.0%

Ease of research Library website * first-years vs. fourth-years Crosstabulation

		first-years vs. fourth-years		Total
		first-year students	fourth-year students	
eLibrary website	very difficult	4.5%	2.7%	3.7%
	difficult	10.8%	13.1%	11.8%
	average	34.1%	37.6%	35.5%
	easy	29.6%	33.9%	31.4%
	very easy	21.0%	12.7%	17.6%
Total		100.0%	100.0%	100.0%

Ease of research OU Website * first-years vs. fourth-years Crosstabulation

		first-years vs. fourth-years		Total
		first-year students	fourth-year students	
eOU Website	very difficult	13.9%	20.5%	16.5%
	difficult	16.5%	16.1%	16.3%
	average	30.4%	30.2%	30.3%
	easy	21.8%	21.5%	21.7%
	very easy	17.5%	11.7%	15.2%
Total		100.0%	100.0%	100.0%

Ease of research Google Scholar * first-years vs. fourth-years Crosstabulation

		first-years vs. fourth-years		Total
		first-year students	fourth-year students	
eGoogle Scholar	very difficult	4.6%	2.2%	3.7%
	difficult	13.8%	8.9%	11.9%
	average	29.0%	31.9%	30.1%
	easy	32.3%	34.1%	33.0%
	very easy	20.3%	23.0%	21.3%
Total		100.0%	100.0%	100.0%

Ease of research EBSCO * first-years vs. fourth-years Crosstabulation

		first-years vs. fourth-years		Total
		first-year students	fourth-year students	
eEBSCO	very difficult	4.3%	4.8%	4.5%
	difficult	14.6%	7.7%	11.9%
	average	37.9%	46.4%	41.3%
	easy	26.9%	29.2%	27.8%
	very easy	16.2%	11.9%	14.5%
Total		100.0%	100.0%	100.0%

Ease of research InfoTree * first-years vs. fourth-years Crosstabulation

		first-years vs. fourth-years		Total
		first-year students	fourth-year students	
eInfoTree	very difficult	4.8%	3.5%	4.2%
	difficult	16.1%	12.4%	14.4%
	average	33.7%	36.6%	35.0%
	easy	28.9%	30.2%	29.5%
	very easy	16.5%	17.3%	16.9%
Total		100.0%	100.0%	100.0%

Ease of research Article database or index * first-years vs. fourth-years Crosstabulation

		first-years vs. fourth-years		
		first-year students	fourth-year students	Total
eArticle database or index	very difficult	3.9%	3.7%	3.8%
	difficult	20.2%	11.8%	16.7%
	average	33.5%	41.2%	36.7%
	easy	26.1%	32.1%	28.6%
	very easy	16.3%	11.2%	14.2%
Total		100.0%	100.0%	100.0%

Quality of Wikipedia * first-years vs. fourth-years Crosstabulation

		first-years vs. fourth-years		
		first-year students	fourth-year students	Total
qWikipedia	poor	18.1%	13.3%	16.1%
	fair	20.0%	29.2%	23.8%
	average	27.5%	29.6%	28.4%
	good	23.1%	20.4%	22.0%
	excellent	11.3%	7.5%	9.7%
Total		100.0%	100.0%	100.0%

Quality of Google * first-years vs. fourth-years Crosstabulation

		first-years vs. fourth-years		
		first-year students	fourth-year students	Total
qGoogle	poor	2.0%	3.3%	2.6%
	fair	12.1%	13.0%	12.5%
	average	28.0%	31.4%	29.4%
	good	32.7%	34.3%	33.3%
	excellent	25.1%	18.0%	22.2%
Total		100.0%	100.0%	100.0%

Quality of ALICE * first-years vs. fourth-years Crosstabulation

		first-years vs. fourth-years		
		first-year students	fourth-year students	Total
qALICE	poor	3.2%	.9%	2.2%
	fair	1.6%	3.9%	2.6%
	average	23.0%	16.6%	20.3%
	good	42.2%	51.1%	45.9%
	excellent	30.0%	27.5%	29.0%
Total		100.0%	100.0%	100.0%

Quality of Academic Search Complete * first-years vs. fourth-years Crosstabulation

		first-years vs. fourth-years		Total
		first-year students	fourth-year students	
qAcademic Search Complete	poor	4.6%	1.1%	3.2%
	fair	2.7%	2.7%	2.7%
	average	21.2%	15.8%	19.0%
	good	39.4%	45.4%	41.9%
	excellent	32.0%	35.0%	33.3%
Total		100.0%	100.0%	100.0%

Quality of Library website * first-years vs. fourth-years Crosstabulation

		first-years vs. fourth-years		Total
		first-year students	fourth-year students	
qLibrary website	poor	3.0%	[err]	1.7%
	fair	3.9%	6.4%	5.0%
	average	26.6%	34.4%	29.9%
	good	41.1%	42.2%	41.6%
	excellent	25.3%	17.0%	21.8%
Total		100.0%	100.0%	100.0%

Quality of OU Website * first-years vs. fourth-years Crosstabulation

		first-years vs. fourth-years		Total
		first-year students	fourth-year students	
qOU Website	poor	8.2%	12.5%	10.0%
	fair	10.6%	20.5%	14.6%
	average	30.1%	33.0%	31.3%
	good	33.2%	26.0%	30.3%
	excellent	17.8%	8.0%	13.8%
Total		100.0%	100.0%	100.0%

Appendix C: Correlation Scales and Measures

Academic Status 1: undergraduate, 2: graduate

Age 1: 17-19, 2: 20-22, 3: 23-26, 4: 27-30, 5: >31

Digital Status 1: digital native, 2: digital immigrant

Library Visits 1: never, 2: monthly, 3: weekly, 4: several times a week, 5: daily

Library Web Visits 1: never, 2: monthly, 3: weekly, 4: several times a week, 5: daily

Time Online (hours per week) – 1: <5, 2: 6-10, 3: 11-20, 4: 21-40, 5: 31-40, 6: >40

Academic Time Online 1: none, 2: less than 25%, 3: about half, 4: more 75%, 5: most

Technology Skill average of word processing, presentation, computer troubleshooting, media software, web editing, and blackboard skills on a 1-5 scale into 1: least skilled, 2: somewhat skilled, 3: moderately skilled, 4: very skilled, 5: most skilled

Library/Research Skill average of finding books and articles and using library resources for research on a 1-5 scale, 1: least skilled, 2: somewhat skilled, 3: moderately skilled, 4: very skilled, 5: most skilled

Technology Adoption recoded 5-part tech adoption scale, 1: late, 2: mainstream, 3: early

Social Software Use 1-8 scale of specific social technologies used

Technology Ownership 1-10 scale of specific information and communication tools owned

Library Technology Receptivity mean of receptivity to Facebook applications, MySpace applications, library toolbars, web calling, text messaging, and mobile browsing services into 1: not receptive, 2: somewhat receptive, 3: very receptive

About the Author

Char Booth is E-Learning Librarian at the University of California at Berkeley, and was previously a Reference and Instruction Librarian at Ohio University from 2006-2008. A 2007 ALA Emerging Leader and 2008 *Library Journal* Mover and Shaker, Char advocates for library cultures of experimentation and assessment, free and open source solutions to library sustainability, and instructional design and pedagogical training in library education. She completed a Masters (MEd) in Computer Education and Technology at Ohio University in 2008, a MSIS at the University of Texas at Austin School of Information in 2005, and a BA in History at Reed College in Portland, Oregon, in 2001. Char blogs about library futures and technology literacy at *www.infomational.com*, and her publications can be found in *Library Journal*, the *Journal of Access Services*, the *Internet Reference Services Quarterly*, and as Technology Column Editor for the *Public Services Quarterly*. Char can be reached at charbooth@gmail.com.

Photos, illustrations, layout, and cover design by Char Booth.

Typefaces: Arial | ORATOR STD | andale mono | Apple LiGothic Medium | Apple Myungjo | OCR A Std